Planning Additions to Academic Library Buildings

A Seamless Approach

edited by
Pat Hawthorne and Ron G. Martin

Based on a program sponsored by the
Buildings for College and University Libraries Committee
of the Buildings and Equipment Section, a section of the
Library Administration and Management Association

American Library Association
Chicago and London
1995

Project Manager: Joan A. Grygel

Cover design: Tessing Design

Composition by Dianne M. Rooney in Cheltenham and Franklin
    Gothic using QuarkXpress 3.3 for the Macintosh 7100/66

Printed on 60-pound Torch Glow Colonial White, a pH-neutral
    stock, and bound in 10-point C1S cover stock by
    Commercial Communications, Inc.

The paper used in this publication meets the minimum
requirements of American National Standard for Information
Sciences—Permanence of Paper for Printed Library Materials,
ANSI Z39.48-1992. ∞

Library of Congress Cataloging-in-Publication Data
Planning additions to academic library buildings : a
    seamless approach / Pat Hawthorne and Ron G. Martin, editors.
        p.   cm.
    ISBN 0-8389-0651-6
    1. Library architecture—United States.   2. Buildings—
Additions—United States—Planning.   3. Academic
libraries—United States.
I. Hawthorne, Pat.   II. Martin, Ron G.
Z679.5.P57   1995
727'.8'0973—dc20   95-14005

Printed in the United States of America.

99 98 97 96 95   5 4 3 2 1

CONTENTS

Preface   v

Acknowledgments   vii

Introduction
     Carolyn A. Snyder   ix

CASE STUDY 1

Van Wylen Library, Hope College
     An Addition That Became a New Building
          David Jensen and Margaret Jensen   xii

CASE STUDY 2

Hoover Library, Western Maryland College
     Growth Creates Need for a "New" Hoover Library
          Dave Neikirk   16

CASE STUDY 3

Kenneth S. Allen Library, University of Washington
     Planning a Main Library Addition for an Academic
     Research Library
          Sarah C. Michalak   28

Summary   45

Appendixes
A. Poster Session Abstracts   *Ron G. Martin*   47
B. Checklist of Additions to Academic Library Buildings
     Nancy McAdams   53
C. Bibliography of Related ALA/LAMA Publications
     64

PREFACE

Growing paper collections, expanding technology, new services and programs, and rising user expectations all combine to create more demands on academic library buildings. Increasingly, the solution to the pressing need for more space is being met not by entirely new buildings but by additions to existing buildings.

Many academic institutions planning library building additions seek the "seamless" addition to expand, modify, and enhance an existing structure while creating an environment that is pleasing to the eye as well as one that is accessible, functional, and inviting.

Planning such a seamless architectural solution involves more than enlarging an existing structure. As many librarians know, additions bring with them their own set of issues and concerns—site considerations, financial constraints, aesthetics, and function.

Three case studies in this book illustrate how library staffs and architectural design teams can work closely together to plan seamless additions that are successful solutions to building problems.

We are pleased to present this publication that began as a good idea, went on to become a conference program presented at the 1993 Annual Conference of the American Library Association in New Orleans, and has emerged as a title in the *LAMA Occasional Paper Series*.

PAT HAWTHORNE
RON G. MARTIN

ACKNOWLEDGMENTS

This publication exists as a direct result of the time and effort of a number of talented and dedicated individuals in the Library Administration and Management Association of the American Library Association. The editors wish to acknowledge the contributions of these individuals.

Philip J. Tramdack, Editor
Catherine Doyle, Associate Editor
LAMA Occasional Paper Series

Buildings for College and University Libraries Committee
Buildings and Equipment Section

Publications Committee
Buildings and Equipment Section

Publications Committee
Library Administration and Management Association

In addition, we gratefully acknowledge the use of photographs and illustrations provided by Hope College, Western Maryland College, and the University of Washington in their respective case studies.

INTRODUCTION

Discussions of academic library building additions by the Buildings for College and University Libraries Committee (BCUL) of the Library Administration and Management Association (LAMA) led to the 1993 Annual Conference program, "Planning Academic Library Building Additions: A Seamless Approach." This *LAMA Occasional Paper* includes three case studies presented at that program. In addition, Appendix A presents a summary of the program poster sessions, and Appendix B provides a checklist of additions to academic library buildings.

Don Kelsey's introductory remarks as program keynote speaker at the ALA/LAMA program reflect the BCUL's conclusions that many library buildings no longer are capable of meeting the demands placed on them. Collections grow beyond the space allotted to them, encroaching on other areas of the library. Electronic information technology brings with it more hardware and increased need for telecommunications capacity. Staff areas are shifted to accommodate larger collections and new equipment, often becoming cramped, unpleasant, and inefficient work areas in the process. Access and work space for disabled users and staff are added to buildings with serious limitations, not constructed with accessibility for the physically challenged in mind. As academic libraries traverse a period of intense changes, it becomes painfully apparent that new directions and missions require more space, new buildings, renovations, or additions.

When they were built, most library buildings were very serviceable, well designed, and well suited to the needs of the time, according to Kelsey, a leading expert on the planning and design of library facilities and additions. Buildings and their occupants, however, experience incredible stresses throughout their "useful lifetimes." A consequence of the real economic pressures felt by academic institutions is that existing buildings—libraries included—are kept in service far longer than originally intended. When needs must finally be addressed, the solution is often an addition to an existing structure rather than an entirely new building.

To be successful, the addition to an academic library building must be "seamless." Sarah C. Michalak (see Case Study 3) describes a seamless addition as one "in which the architectural design, floor plan, and support functions, such as climate control, pedestrian traffic ways, and elevators, all work together to create a safe, easy-to-maintain, adaptable, pleasing, and scholarly environment for collections, technology, staff, and users." Planning such a seamless architectural solution involves more than the enlarging of an existing structure. Additions involve their own set of issues and concerns, such as site considerations, financial constraints, aesthetics, and functionality.

The case studies presented herein demonstrate that successful, seamless academic library additions are possible. Three individual additions made to distinctly different types of university and college libraries illustrate building additions that so elegantly integrate themselves with the original structures that, for building users, it feels as though building and addition are one.

The case studies present the experiences of Hope College (Holland, Michigan), Western Maryland College (Westminster, Maryland), and the University of Washington (Seattle, Washington). Each study shows the unique requirements of the individual institution as well as the need for successful cooperation among architects, campus planners, consultants, and librarians. The focus of both the ALA/LAMA conference program and this book is on the planning process and the work involved in rethinking library services and operations. Staff at each of the case-study institutions dealt with unique issues, problems, and concerns; yet their experiences can provide inspiration and perspective to other librarians facing similar circumstances.

For success the planning process must include a thorough grasp of site considerations, a review of all library services and functions, and the involvement of library staff. The case studies highlight various considerations in addressing site issues. Library buildings are often centrally positioned on the campus, and they are designed as much for the symbolic statement as they are for function. A very good original site choice has the potential to be troublesome when the fundamental exterior appearance of the building is changed by the addition.

Along with the location of the building and its relationship to its surroundings, the planner must consider the whole set of issues of how people come to the building. How will the building, with its addition, affect established traffic patterns in the surrounding space? Just as the functions that a library building supports are continuously evolving, the configuration of the buildings and spaces that surround the library also change. Over the years a traffic pattern that was suitable when the building was erected may have been seriously disrupted by other more-recent structures in its proximity. Thus, an addition can present a golden opportunity to rethink how people approach the library and to correct problems that have developed outside the building in the course of time.

Library staff can almost always describe what they do in their day-to-day activity. However, the architect's role is to work with the staff to understand their functions in spatial terms and to clarify future needs. The following case studies show ways in which the organization of spaces and functions changed between the original building and the finished project. Many times the ultimate success of a library addition depends as much on the staff's willingness to examine critically the library's physical organization as it does on the architect's contribution to the process.

The first case study is Van Wylen Library at Hope College, a project in which a new structure was added onto the original building. The seamlessness of this addition results, in part, from a major rethinking of the organization and arrangement of functions in the expanded building.

The second case study, Hoover Library at Western Maryland College, features an addition so completely integrated into the original structure that now it is virtually impossible to know where the original structure begins and ends.

The third example is the University of Washington Library, a situation in which every aspect of the project seemed to conspire against seamlessness. The original structure was confusing and had three previous additions. Because of an engineering concern, only the smallest openings would be permitted between the old structure and the new. Finally, the design team was constrained by an extremely problematic site and a project budget insufficient to correct the severe organizational and structural problems of the old building. Yet, the project succeeded in creating a greatly improved main library building that operates as a whole in harmony with its site and surroundings.

These three case studies illustrate how a library staff and an architectural design team can work closely together to plan seamless additions that are successful solutions to complex space requirements in a time of unprecedented library change and equally problematic fiscal realities.

CAROLYN A. SNYDER
Chair, 1993 Program Committee
Buildings for College and University Libraries Committee
Buildings and Equipment Section
Library Administration and Management Association

An Addition That Became a New Building

David Jensen and
Margaret Jensen

Van Wylen Library, Hope College

Hope College's Van Zoeren Library simply outgrew itself.
Hope, a four-year liberal arts college, is located two blocks
from downtown Holland, Michigan, on the eastern shore of
Lake Michigan. Situated on the western edge of the campus, the Van
Zoeren Library was dedicated in 1961. At that time its facilities and
37,000 square feet were more than ample to serve the college's 1,500
students and to house the 50,000-volume collection.

Over the next 21 years, however, the college's enrollment grew
to 2,200 students, and the collection nearly quintupled to more than
245,000 volumes. The need to accommodate the increasing size of
the collection had resulted in a number of "Band-Aid" solutions familiar to librarians facing the inexorable growth of collections, staff,
and services. To make way for book stacks, study seating was pro-
gressively reduced on all three levels of the library, and an audiovisual classroom was eliminated. The librarian's office on the first
floor was transformed into the OCLC terminal room. Seminar rooms
were sacrificed, partitioned, and converted to staff offices, and the
Special Collections Room became a classroom.

In 1982 the college's administration began considering an expansion of the Van Zoeren Library, a two-story modular structure with
basement. The first step was the formation of a library planning
committee that was assigned the task of finding more space for
materials, readers, staff, and services.

Library Planning Committee Begins Work

Although the need for additional space was the primary focus of
the library planning committee, four other areas of concern required
its attention: thermal efficiency, lighting, ambiance, and site selection.

In the architectural style typical of the 1960s, the Van Zoeren
Library was designed with glass walls of single-pane windows on the
northern, western, and southern exposures. The sunlight that entered
through these extensive window areas was unbroken except by a
brick lattice screen on the second floor. The result was excessive
heat gain in the summer and heat loss in the winter as well as solar
damage to some library materials. The lack of air conditioning com-
pounded the thermal inefficiency of the building. The library plan-

ning committee decided to seek a design that would provide efficient heating, cooling, and ventilation.

Another task the committee undertook was to improve lighting. The library's large 4-foot by 4-foot fluorescent fixtures installed at wide intervals provided uneven lighting in stack areas.

A further goal of the library planning committee was to ensure that the ambiance of the library be warm and welcoming, making it a place that Hope College students would want to use. The Van Zoeren Library was crowded and projected an atmosphere of sterility. The building also featured a mezzanine with a centrally located opening, permitting noise from circulation, reference, and photocopy areas to rise from the first floor to the second. Quiet study on either floor was nearly impossible.

Finally, the library planning committee needed to locate an appropriate site for either an addition or an entirely new building. Site selection is crucial in any library building project because it affects campus planning, shape and size of the building, placement of the entrance, exterior design, and location of internal functions. The committee rejected suggestions for a new library closer to the center of campus for a number of reasons. In one case, the proposed location would have forced the moving of the President's House, a historic structure. In another case, a location in close proximity to dormitories was considered and dismissed because it would have modified the library's identity so that its function as a place of learning would have been partially eclipsed by its importance as a social center.

Instead, the option selected was one recommended by Paul Sun and Geoffrey Freeman, architects from the Boston firm of Shepley, Bulfinch, Richardson and Abbott. Sun and Freeman recommended building onto the east side of the Van Zoeren Library where the land presented the best opportunity for a structure of the size required. The selection of this site was complicated by the fact that Hope College did not own all of the land it proposed to use. Dr. Gordon Van Wylen, the college president at that time, was concerned that the Hope College Board of Trustees would not approve the land purchase since the owners were asking double the estimated value. However, the chairperson of the board felt it was not worth delaying an $8.5 million project for $100,000. The board approved the purchase.

The size and configuration of the site for the new library, as in every building project, was limited by existing buildings, streets, and geological factors. The plot east of Van Zoeren was bordered by three streets, calling for a long, rectangular building. Furthermore, the local water table was approximately four feet under the basement floor, making it impossible to construct more than one story underground. Because of this constraint and the amount of space needed in the new building, the architects had to find a design that would minimize the size of the structure above ground so that it would not dwarf the surrounding buildings. Finally, the soil was sandy and required compaction every place a column foundation pad was to be constructed.

Architects Propose "New" Library

In reality, what the architects proposed was not really an addition but a new library of five stories and 92,000 square feet. The architects envisioned the new library as the focal point of an integrated complex of four buildings that would enhance the western side of the campus and keep the library's identity as a center for learning intact. According to the architects' proposal, the Van Zoeren Library Building would be physically joined to Vander Werf Hall, the physics and mathematics building to the west of Van Zoeren, as well as to the new library. The architects' design would also create a visual link between the new library and Peale Science Center to its south. (See figure 1.)

The architects further recommended that the basement be the only portion of Van Zoeren to remain a part of the library; the first and second floors would be remodeled for use as classrooms and faculty offices. The architects' plan provided for future expansion by proposing that materials or services be moved back into the old library building when the new one became too crowded. Ironically, not only had the addition become a new building but the old building would eventually become a new addition.

New Library Seeks Name and Identity

The new library needed a name and a distinct identity. Naming the library provided an opportunity to honor Dr. Gordon Van Wylen, then the current president of the college, who was preparing to retire. One of the ways in which the architects gave the new library an identity all its own was by departing radically from the architectural style of Van Zoeren. Although Vander Werf Hall mirrored the exterior design of Van Zoeren Library and the Peale Science Center reflected the "fortress" mentality of the 1970s, the architects chose

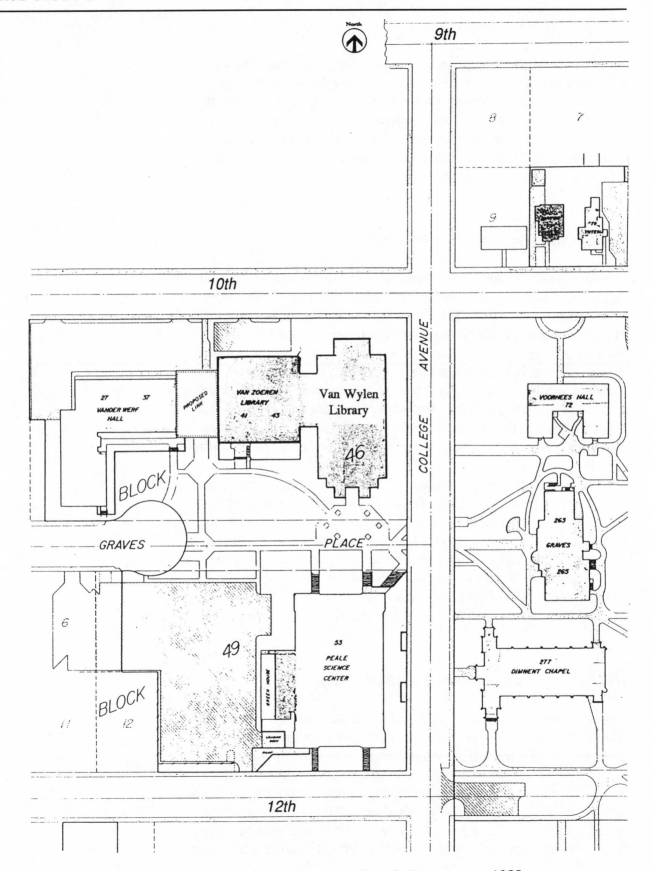

FIGURE 1. Master site plan of west end of Hope College campus, 1988

as their inspiration for the new Van Wylen Library two earlier Dutch-style buildings in close proximity to the site.

The key elements of this Dutch style—brick broken by stone bands, steeply pitched roofs, and stepped gables—were incorporated into Van Wylen's design through the use of stepped windows suggesting the stepped gables. Furthermore, the visual mass of the structure is broken up by the liberal use of dormers. Inside, the dormers and roof cuts produce many interesting nooks and crannies that readers find inviting and conducive to study.

Architect Paul Sun said he had always wanted to design a Dutch building with a Chinese twist. The Chinese twist in this case is the use of light. For example, a skylight over the central staircase brings light into the center of the building through the glass walls enclosing the stairs. Openings between the floors, sealed with glass, let natural light reach reading areas and permit visual connections from one floor to another while eliminating noise between levels. This design effectively combined natural and artificial sources of light to illuminate all areas of the library without allowing the light in any of the areas to become harsh. These factors have been instrumental in making Van Wylen a comfortable and inviting library.

Functional Changes Help Create "New" Library

Determining the location of the entrance to the new library emerged as a campus-planning issue. The architects sought to link the entrance directly to the campus without the intervention of a street. College Avenue, the street bordering the long side of the building and a major north-south artery in Holland, was eliminated as an option for the entrance. However, Graves Place to the south was only one block long, and by closing the portion that lay between the proposed addition and the Peale Science Center, a connection was created between the two buildings. The entrance to the new library is situated on the south end and opened onto a newly constructed pedestrian plaza.

Despite a four-foot elevation on the first floor, a ground-level entrance was constructed, making access to Van Wylen inviting and convenient. The stairs and ramp necessary to move users from the entrance to the first floor were simply placed inside the building, a major plus during Michigan winters with their frequent and significant snowfall. Enclosing the stairs and ramp provided an additional opportunity to set aside space for a student lounge, which has proven to be a popular and useful adjunct to the library.

First Floor

As one moves from the lobby/lounge area into the library itself, the reference desk is located immediately to the right. Reference had occupied a hidden location in Van Zoeren Library, but in the new Van Wylen Library, the security gate at the main entry was designed to point patrons directly toward the reference desk, making it a natural focal point.

The decision to situate the entrance at one end of Van Wylen complicated the layout of the reference collection, making it necessary to place the most-distant portion of the collection ninety feet away from the entrance. Despite this complication, the relocation of reference is perhaps the most-significant and certainly one of the most-positive functional changes made with the construction of Van Wylen.

Opposite the reference desk is circulation, in the same relative position as it was in the old building. The circulation service area was substantially increased to provide room for built-in shelving to accommodate reserves, additional and larger staff work stations, and a long counter to process returned materials. (See figure 2.)

Planning of the reference area and the entire first floor was simplified by the knowledge that the card catalog would be replaced by an online public access catalog soon after the opening of the new library. The idea of installing an integrated automation system in the library was an important element in the building program. An automation plan was developed and, as a result, a bank of public access catalog terminals was placed near the reference desk. Additional terminals were installed in visible and high-traffic areas on every floor.

The plan to automate presented an opportunity to wire the building completely so that every service desk, office, group study room, private study, and built-in carrel would be equipped with data and communications lines for future use of computers.

As with reference, the position of interlibrary loans was also significantly improved, relocating from the technical services area to its own space within the reference office.

Technical services in Van Wylen also remained in the same relative position as it had been in Van Zoeren—on the west side of the first floor. The department's floor space was increased substantially to allow the entire technical services staff to be located in one area, and the layout of the department was totally reorganized to improve productivity.

Current periodicals in Van Wylen Library are housed on the north end of the first floor. This location makes them easier to find than they had been in the old library, where they were housed on

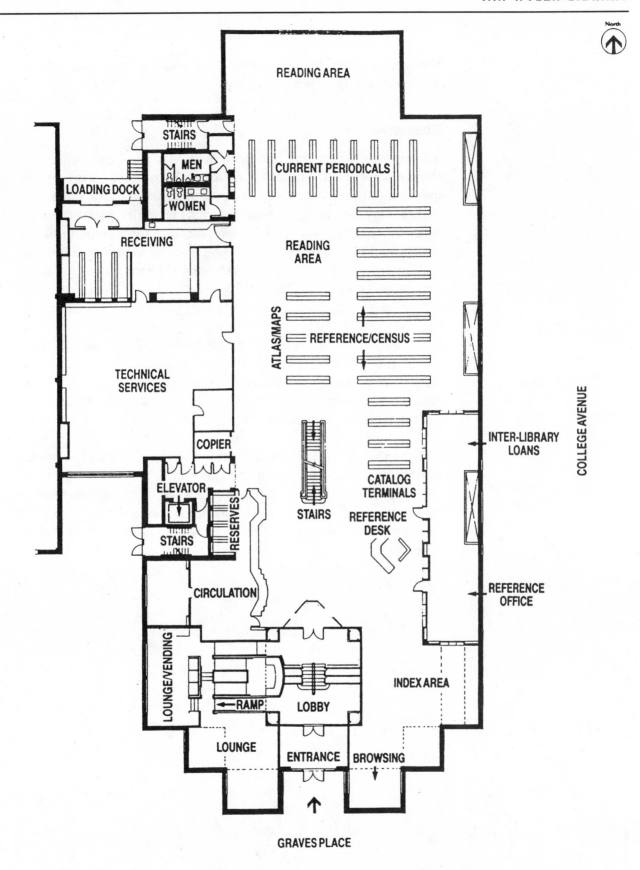

FIGURE 2. Van Wylen Library, first floor

the second floor. New display shelving was designed and custom manufactured for the new library.

Basement

The science library that had been housed in the Peale Science Center was closed, and all the materials it contained were reintegrated into the main collection. As a concession to the chemistry and biology faculty, the science journals were not shelved with other current periodicals but were placed in the basement of Van Wylen so they would be on the same floor as the science indexes and abstracts. This was a relatively easy division to make since serials are classified at Hope College.

Archives is the only function that remained in the same place, the west end of the basement of the Van Zoeren Building. However, it was expanded to more than twice its original size, and the rare books and special collections that had been housed on the second floor of Van Zoeren were moved to the basement to occupy a new rare book room that also serves as the entrance and reading room for the archives. (See figure 3.)

All the mechanical rooms serving both the Van Zoeren Building and the Van Wylen Library are located in Van Zoeren's basement, permitting the newly constructed space in Van Wylen to be employed solely for library purposes. The space shared by the basements of Van Zoeren and Van Wylen is so seamless that most patrons using the basement cannot tell whether they are standing in the old or new library.

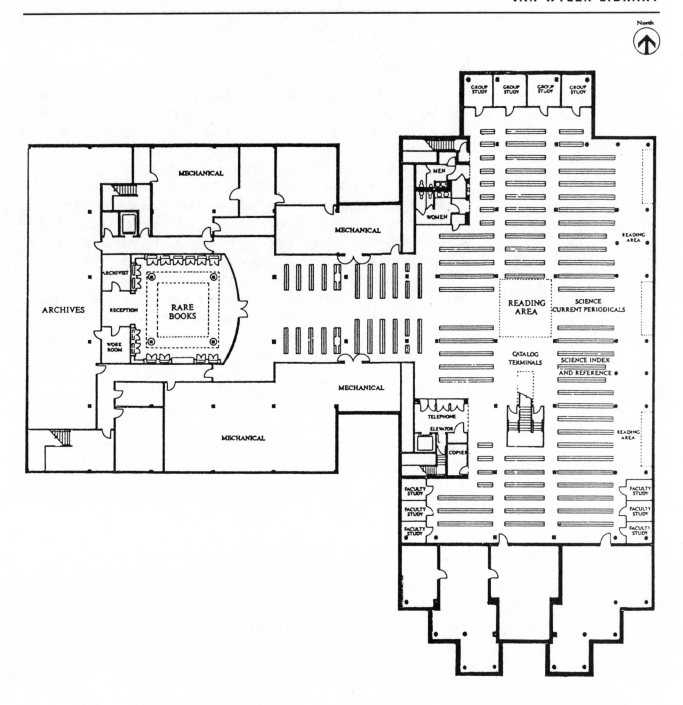

North

FIGURE 3. Van Zoeren/Van Wylen, basement

Second Floor

On the second floor, an entrance links Van Zoeren, now a classroom building, and Van Wylen Library, making it possible to walk from the Vander Werf Hall, the physics and mathematics building, through Van Zoeren to Van Wylen without going outside. This has resulted in an enormous increase of foot traffic through the library.

The curriculum library and the media center are located just within the second floor entrance because the planners foresaw moving the education department to the second floor of the renovated Van Zoeren Building. (See figure 4.) The center contains a full-service circulation desk, and individuals who staff this desk must be ready to assist readers using a number of different resources: the curriculum library, the instructional media center, microforms, microcomputers, and audiovisual materials and equipment. Relocating the curriculum library and instructional media center from the basement of Van Zoeren to a highly visible location in close proximity to the education department has greatly increased the use of these service areas and the resources they house.

A specially designed classroom, the Granberg Room, is located within sight of the second floor circulation desk. Intended for bibliographic instruction, it has become one of the most sought-after rooms on campus.

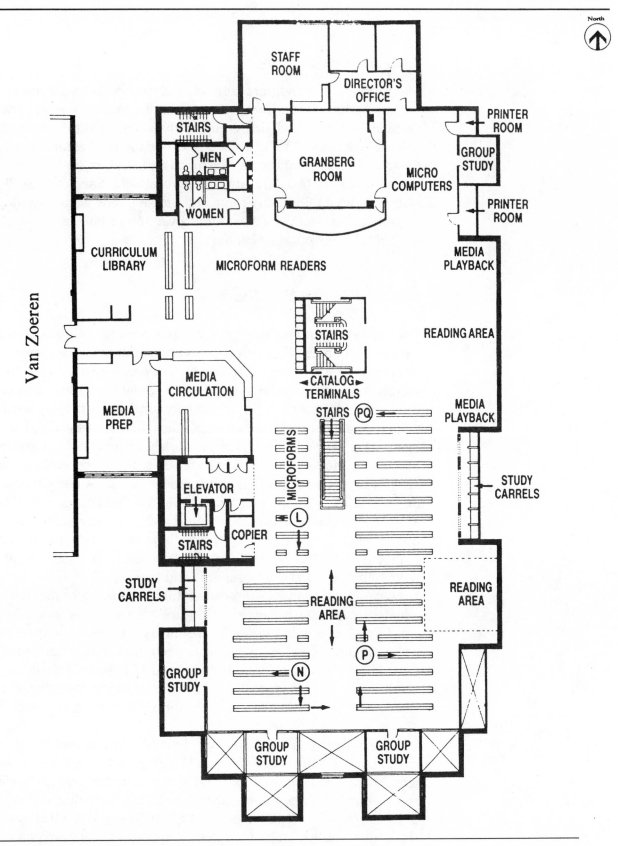

Note: Circled letters refer to Library of Congress classification and location in the stacks.

FIGURE 4. Van Wylen Library, second floor

Third and Fourth Floors

The third and fourth floors contain book stacks and a variety of seating options for readers—carrels built in under the eaves, traditional tables, casual chairs, group study rooms, and private studies. (See figures 5 and 6.) The book stacks occupy the center sections of these two floors, and the seating areas and studies are located on the periphery to take advantage of natural light. Each of these floors also includes a photocopy room and online public access catalog terminals. The fourth floor features a vaulted ceiling and attractive views of the surrounding campus.

Success Is the End Result

The success of any building project rests on contributions from a variety of sources. While everyone's contributions were important, the library staff's suggestions and ideas were instrumental to the architects in creating the friendly, inviting ambiance that has made the biggest difference in library activity. One factor helping to produce this ambiance is the variety of study spaces designed to accommodate the tastes and needs of the library's users. Individual carrels built under the eaves offer cozy, enclosed study space, and the casual seating areas by the windows offer readers a more-open environment. In addition, fourteen group studies and sixteen private studies are scattered throughout the building, many of them located in the dormers that provide an interesting shape and feel. Warm hues predominate in the study areas and were chosen by the staff and architects to provide a sense of comfort and ease.

Given the improved and newly established services and the wonderfully cordial atmosphere of Van Wylen, it was reasonable to expect an increase in the use of the library. However, the increased use of the library far exceeded all expectations. Since Van Wylen opened in 1988, circulation has increased 75 percent, reference questions have tripled, cash photocopies have increased by 40 percent, and even the demand for interlibrary borrowing has risen by 43 percent.

A positive attitude on the part of staff, students, and faculty was essential in making the move from Van Zoeren to Van Wylen seamless. People on campus responded with excitement and enthusiasm to the opening of the library, almost as if they were discovering for the first time that Hope College had a fine library. It is a testimony to the efforts of the staff that services in the new library are perceived

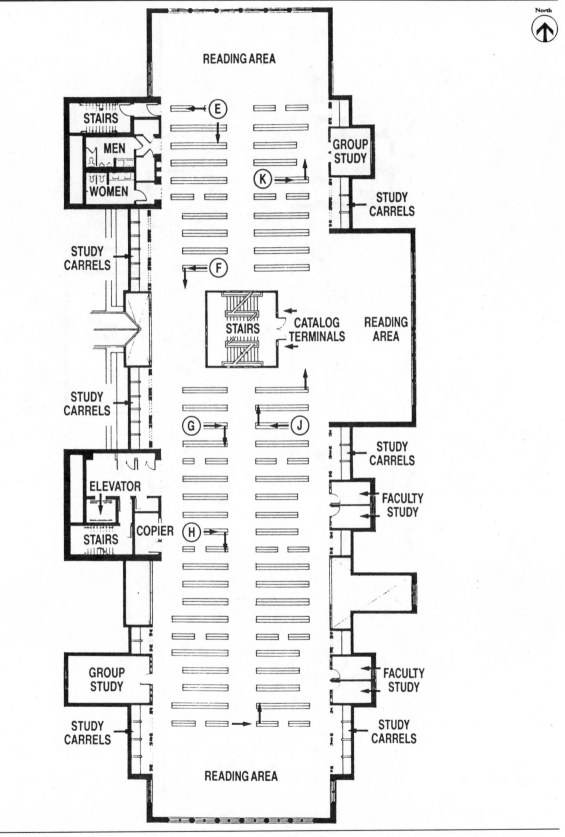

Note: Circled letters refer to Library of Congress classification and location in the stacks.

FIGURE 5. Van Wylen Library, third floor

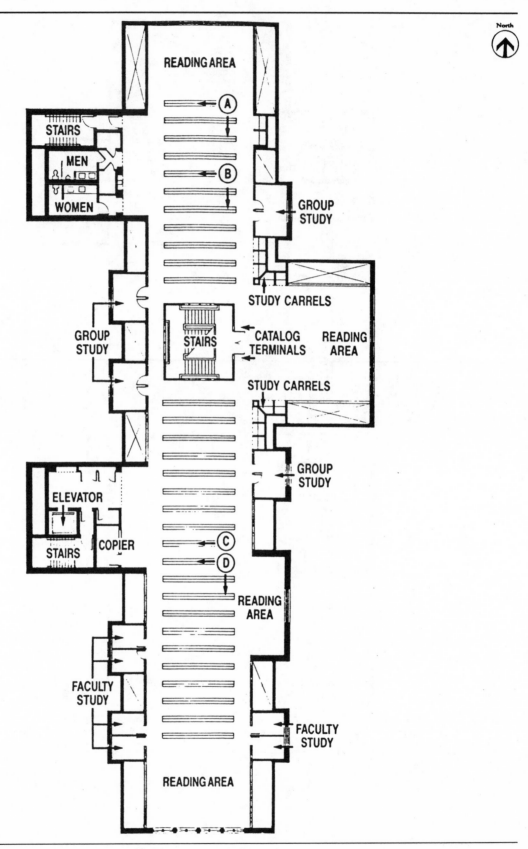

Note: Circled letters refer to Library of Congress classification and location in the stacks.

FIGURE 6. Van Wylen Library, fourth floor

as being vastly improved, which is true in many cases. It is a testimony to the vision of the planners and designers that everything in the building is perceived almost universally as being better. After the building had been open a few months, the chairperson of the library planning committee remarked that "even the books look better."

As had been hoped, a large increase in traffic to the western part of the campus occurred after the addition to the library opened and the renovation of Van Zoeren and Vander Werf was completed. Van Zoeren and Vander Werf were given a new, common facade so they became a single architectural unit. Their style remains very different from the Dutch style adopted for Van Wylen, which stands out as a distinct architectural entity.

The library "addition" that became a new building has a commanding physical presence and a clear and powerful identity as an intellectual and cultural center of Hope College.

Growth Creates Need for a "New" Hoover Library

Dave Neikirk

Hoover Library

Western Maryland College

Forty-four years after its founding in 1867, Western Maryland College built its first library. The 1911 building served the small, independent liberal arts college in north central Maryland for fifty years and was replaced in 1961 by a new building, named to honor Dr. Samuel Hoover, a local philanthropist.

The 1961 Hoover Library contained 26,000 net assignable square feet and was designed to hold 100,000 volumes and provide 250 user seats, more than adequate for the then approximately 50,000-volume collection and 900 students. The building consisted of four floors built into the side of a hill. Its third floor, counting from the lowest level up, served as the main entry level and was at grade, while the two lower levels were below grade on the uphill side but above grade on the west, or downhill, side. The rectangular building was six bays wide by three bays deep. Its columns were 22.5 feet apart, center to center, and were spaced to provide 36-inch stack aisles. The design intention assumed double-faced book stacks, 18 inches deep and installed 54 inches apart, upright to upright.

Building Is No Longer Functional

By 1987 the Hoover Library was suffering from a severe space deficit. The collection numbered 145,000 volumes (45,000 volumes beyond design capacity) and seating had been reduced to 150 to make room for additional book stacks. Undergraduate enrollment had reached 1,250, and an evening division had been established serving an additional 700 or so nonresident graduate students.

Not only did the existing building lack sufficient space to accommodate collection growth but illogical placement of added shelving units, installed piecemeal, had fragmented library resources and made them difficult to find and use. There were too few study seats for the campus population, and the quality of study space had deteriorated beyond inconvenience to shabbiness and discomfort. Staff work spaces were so badly congested that productivity and morale were adversely affected. Faculty, students, and accrediting agencies considered the library an impediment to academic achievement.

Conditions in 1987, on the eve of planning for the new addition, were far from ideal. The reference librarian sat at a battered old wooden desk. Signage was rudimentary; the largest sign in the building advertised the presence of restrooms one floor down. The workroom was utterly chaotic. A grove of power poles supported essential technology: an OCLC terminal, an IBM PC/XT used by acquisitions, some electric typewriters, a microfiche reader, two electric erasers, a hot plate, and a coffee pot.

Campus opinion held that the original Hoover Library, more than twenty years after its opening, was fundamentally flawed and unable to meet basic functional requirements. A review of the documents, however, showed that its modularity, lighting grid, and overall layout were specified by a highly competent consultant and were logical, efficient, and inherently flexible. Subsequent rearrangements necessitated by collection growth, however, had been implemented without adequate planning or sensitivity to their impact on overall functionalities and had compromised the building's basic design logic.

The building's basic lack of presence did not reflect the architect's intention but was the result of a conscious decision by the college that the library facade not project beyond the sacristy entrance at the rear of adjacent Baker Chapel. At that time the college was affiliated with the Methodist Church, and it was important that the library, which represented secular values, be seen to occupy a subordinate position. After disaffiliation of the church and college in 1975, this view lost currency, and the campus community became increasingly disenchanted by the discrepancy between the big church building and the little library.

College Expands Library

In 1987 a decision was reached to expand the library building and address the need for more space. The Hillier Group of Princeton, New Jersey, was selected as project architect and given the unenviable task of resolving a number of institutional imperatives at apparent cross purposes and on a very tight budget.

The new library was intended to become the dominating physical and symbolic presence at the very center of the campus, but to the library staff, functionality took precedence over appearance. The first priority was to create a seamless and functionally effective union of old and new.

Built directly in front of the 1961 facade, the new library addition totally masks the 1961 building from frontal view. The addition is a square brick building consisting of three floors, all above grade. The building contains 26,000 net assignable square feet, and the combined capacity of the addition and the original structure is 300,000 volumes and 540 seats.

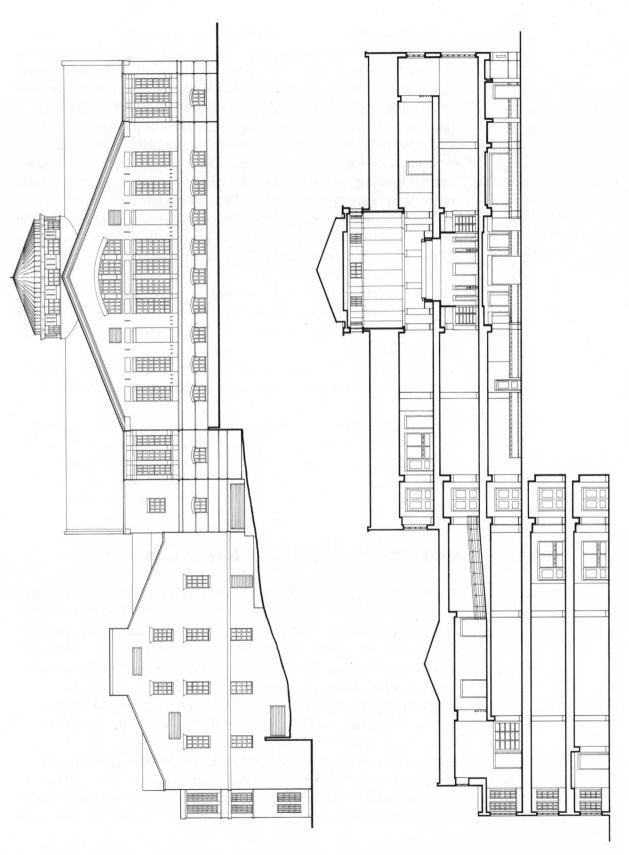

FIGURE 7. Hoover Library, site plan with elevation detail

Between old and new buildings, there are five levels linked by a central stair and an elevator tower. (See figure 7.) The first floor of the new building is at the same elevation as the third floor of the old building and is the main or entry level. Since the new building requires greater slab-to-slab clearance than the original structure, a ramp links the old mezzanine level with the new second floor.

To simplify the transition from new to old, the new building replicates the spacing of the columns and lights established in the original building. Stack ranges are turned 90 degrees, however, eliminating the claustrophobic sense of enclosure characteristic of the old building, where range orientation often blocked sight lines to the building's perimeter. Ranges are placed perpendicular to fluorescent strips and receive uniform illumination regardless of aisle width.

The organizing principle of the floor plan is an east-west axis running from front to back, from new building to old. The architect is fond of calling this the "library street," which provides a uniformity of orientation and layout that was absent in the original building. (See figure 8.)

Main floor services and resources include circulation, the information desk, reference, indexes, and the online public catalog. A public access microcomputer lab and public snack bar, whose doors open off the vestibule but outside library security, can be opened even when the library is closed. Staff offices are on the north and south perimeter, cataloging and acquisitions on the south side served by the existing freight elevator, and reference and interlibrary loan adjacent to the reference collection on the north.

Design Elements Highlight New Library

The building's architectural signature is a central rotunda rising to a rooftop "lantern." On the main floor, the rotunda is a natural traffic hub. The circulation desk, information desk, online catalog, periodical indexes, and reference collections either front onto the rotunda or are in line of sight from it, while the periodical collection is up a single flight of stairs.

In its initial manifestation, the architect proposed that the rotunda be open from street level to the rooftop lantern. Library staff objected to the inevitable introduction of main-floor noise into upper-floor study spaces. The solution was to create a small, elegant rotunda reading room on the second floor. The penetration of the third floor remained as initially proposed, with a custom-built circular study table surrounding it. The two rotunda study areas are

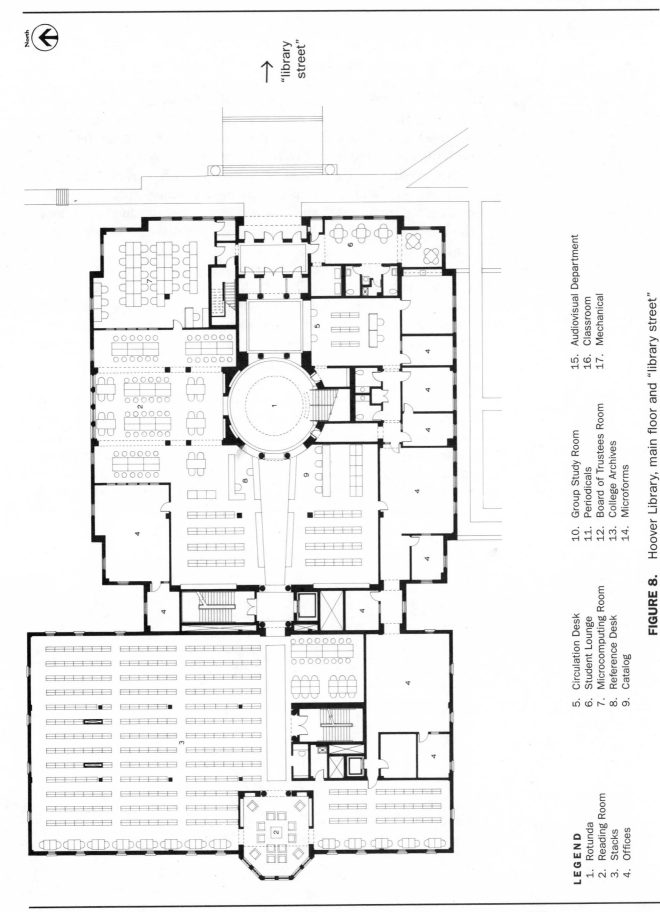

North

↑ "library street"

LEGEND

1. Rotunda
2. Reading Room
3. Stacks
4. Offices
5. Circulation Desk
6. Student Lounge
7. Microcomputing Room
8. Reference Desk
9. Catalog
10. Group Study Room
11. Periodicals
12. Board of Trustees Room
13. College Archives
14. Microforms
15. Audiovisual Department
16. Classroom
17. Mechanical

FIGURE 8. Hoover Library, main floor and "library street"

among the most popular sites in the library; they are attractive, convenient, and quiet—everything that an atrium is not.

The elevator lobby links the new and old sections of the floor. Although there is a difference in ceiling height of about one foot, the differential is effectively masked, and even library visitors familiar with the old building have to be shown where the dividing line is between old and new. Design details used at the entrance vestibule, service desks, and online catalog terminal counters (paneling, pillars, and ceiling treatments) are repeated at the elevator lobby and along the library street to the bay window reading room added during renovation.

The second floor brings together in a single location current periodicals and their back files, bound and microform volumes. Seating is primarily at tables, allowing sprawl room that is useful for magazines and newspapers, with some soft seating also provided. The college archives and library special collections and a large and elegant conference room lie appropriately at the head of the rotunda staircase.

The central east-west axis is interrupted by the rotunda reading room, and the elevation differential between new and old construction requires a ramp. However, the library street is still an effective means of organizing second-floor services. An audiovisual playback area, curriculum center, juvenile literature collection, and lecture room occupy the former mezzanine. By enclosing the space formerly open to the floor below, an attractive and highly functional space has been created. (See figure 9.)

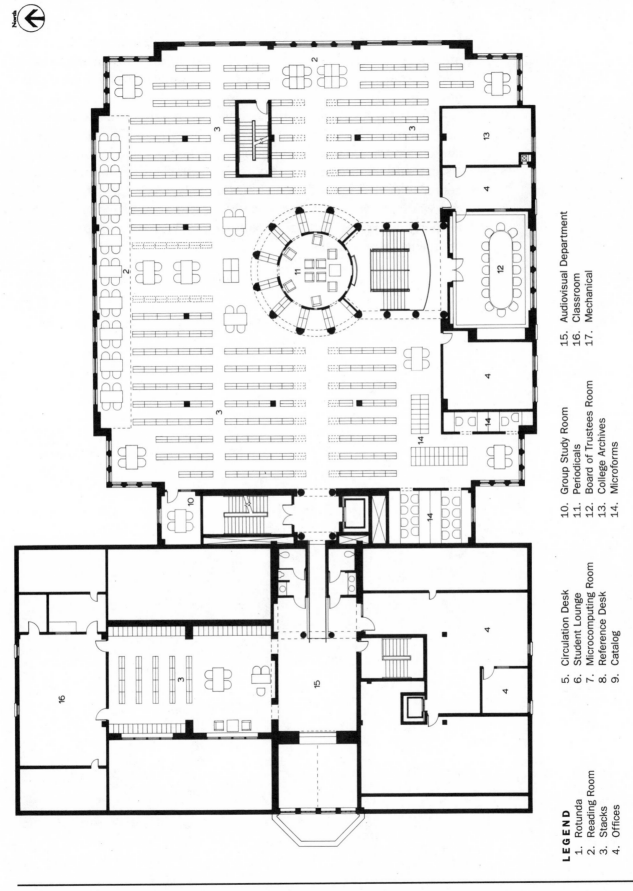

FIGURE 9. Hoover Library, second floor

LEGEND

1. Rotunda
2. Reading Room
3. Stacks
4. Offices
5. Circulation Desk
6. Student Lounge
7. Microcomputing Room
8. Reference Desk
9. Catalog
10. Group Study Room
11. Periodicals
12. Board of Trustees Room
13. College Archives
14. Microforms
15. Audiovisual Department
16. Classroom
17. Mechanical

The addition's third floor is technically a mezzanine because the area opens to the floor below. Group study rooms are located at the floor entrance to make them easy to find and easy to oversee. (See figure 10.)

The lower levels of the old building were gutted during renovation, eliminating a virtual rabbit warren of extraneous walls, doors, and corridors. Entry to these floors and their general layout are consistent with all other library floors. Book stacks were installed in the center of each floor and along interior walls, while the exterior walls and windows were left clear for study space. (See figure 11.) These formerly congested and user-hostile floors were transformed into open and inviting areas.

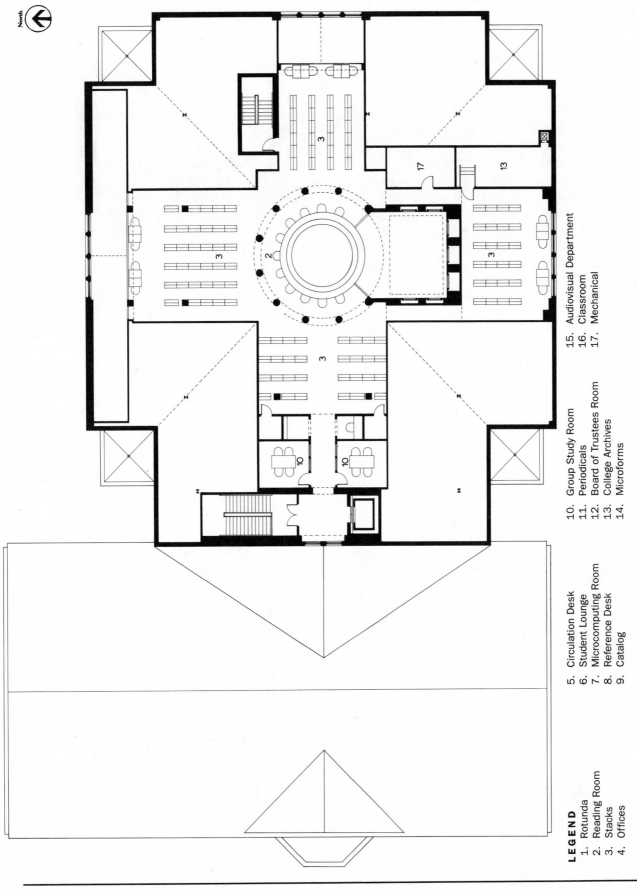

LEGEND

1. Rotunda
2. Reading Room
3. Stacks
4. Offices
5. Circulation Desk
6. Student Lounge
7. Microcomputing Room
8. Reference Desk
9. Catalog
10. Group Study Room
11. Periodicals
12. Board of Trustees Room
13. College Archives
14. Microforms
15. Audiovisual Department
16. Classroom
17. Mechanical

FIGURE 10. Hoover Library, third floor

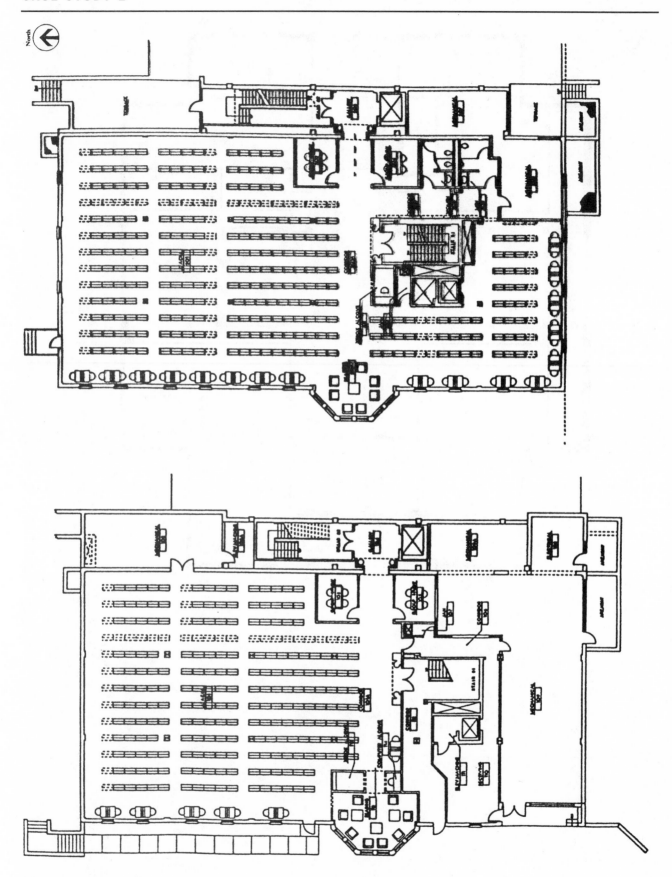

FIGURE 11. Hoover Library, older building lower levels

Campus Community Deems Project Successful

The new library has won the enthusiastic approval of all elements of the campus community. It is the dominant feature of the new college quadrangle and the most elegant building on campus. It is comfortable, well organized, and easy to use. Even librarians, always the severest critics of library design, are happy with the new building because it works so well.

Many elements contributed to the success of the project, especially the ability of Hillier architects Joe Rizzo and Karin Robinson and interior designer Nancy Vargas to balance program requirements and budget realities with architectural vision. The project also benefited from the services of an outstanding general contractor, Henry Lewis Contractors of Owings Mills, Maryland.

To these major determinants we humbly include the decision of the library staff to write the building program for the whole library, not just for the addition to be built. Our initial impulse was to decide which services and resources would be placed in the new building and which would be left relatively untouched in the old. We recognized quite soon that such an approach would perpetuate the improvisational jerry-building that had come to characterize the old building and would waste a unique opportunity to step back and look at the facility as a whole rather than as a loose confederation of parts. Instead, we decided to define adjacency requirements in purely functional terms and to defer placement decisions to the architectural design phase of the project. We think the final results proved we were right to have done so.

Planning a Main Library Addition for an Academic Research Library

Sarah C. Michalak
Kenneth S. Allen Library
University of Washington

At first glance, the 220,000-square-foot Kenneth S. Allen Library does not look like a seamless addition to the University of Washington's Suzzallo Library. Even those involved in planning wondered at times how the space could be successful, either architecturally or functionally, with so many barriers to fulfilling the ultimate goal of fully integrating an addition to the main library. In the end, the skilled library director's vision and determination, the architect and his associates' imaginative and open-minded approach, and the library staff's involvement created a seamless addition that resulted in a main library with 510,000 square feet in four wings.

What is a seamless addition? For me, a seamless library addition is one in which the architectural design, floor plan, and support functions, such as climate control, pedestrian traffic ways, and elevators, all work together to create a safe, easy-to-maintain, adaptable, pleasing, and scholarly environment for collections, technology, staff, and users.

Suzzallo Library Is Part of Early Campus Plan

Serving 32,000 students and located in Seattle beside Lake Washington with a view of Mount Rainier, the University of Washington enjoys a setting of great beauty. To optimize the great advantages of this setting, in 1891 the regents initiated a campus physical-development planning process that continues today to provide a unifying continuity of design across the campus. According to a 1940 publication by John Paul Jones entitled *The History of the Development of the Present Campus Plan for the University of Washington,* the 1915 version of the plan placed the library at the exact center of the campus. This center was at the intersection of three quadrangles, one for the humanities, one for the sciences, and a third between the other two. Around this center quadrangle were the administration, library, and museum—all functions that would serve the entire university. Around the perimeter of the library, major pedestrian pathways connected the library to various segments of the campus.

Two Seattle architects, Carl F. Gould and Charles Bebb, envisioned a triangular shape for the library, with each side of the triangle to be created as the university grew. It was in this early period that the practice of planning additions to the library was consciously adopted, according to the Jones history.

The architectural style of the first two library building wings, built in 1925 and 1935, was Tudor Collegiate Gothic. With light-colored brick, warm-toned terra cotta, green and brown slate tiles for the roof, and decorative statues symbolizing the muses of academe, the building soon became one of the state's architectural treasures. Most of the surrounding structures shared these building materials and, all together, they set the architectural theme for the rest of the university.

In 1963 the university decided to depart from the established theme and experiment with a new look. Architects designed the third library addition—one that reflected the Gothic idea while making a strong contemporary statement with cool glass and concrete modernism. Although the addition was an object of great pride when it opened, it became one of the least-popular structures on campus, a sharp contrast to the mellow traditionalism of other campus structures.

Library Faces Severe Space Shortage

Looking back, we can now see that the 1963 addition was too small almost from the day it was dedicated. At the beginning of the 1960s, planners had envisioned a university and a library to serve 20,000 students. By the beginning of the 1970s, a future population of 30,000 students was projected. In the late 1970s there were at least two major drives on the part of the library staff for additional space based on predictions of considerable shelving shortages by the mid-1980s. Two proposals to solve the problem with off-site storage facilities were not funded.

Director of Libraries Merle Boylan prepared a report for the university administration in 1984 that portrayed the seriousness of the main library's space problems. Although there were seventeen branch libraries in the system with their own incipient space problems, the primary need was for additional space in the Suzzallo Library for the main humanities and social sciences collections. The existing three wings that had been planned for a main library collection of about 500,000 volumes were bursting with twice as many volumes, plus another 1.5 million maps, newspapers, microforms, and government publications.

In his report to the university administration, Boylan emphasized that more than 40 percent of the shelving sections in the building had eight or more shelves on 90-inch uprights, with books on one or more shelves turned onto their fore-edges, causing noticeable collection deterioration. Staff members had adapted conference rooms, closets, and study rooms for collection storage. Boylan's report included more disturbing details. As early as 1972, user seating had been eliminated to add more shelving. Remaining user seats were ill-lighted and too small—frequently including fewer than twelve square feet per work station.

Major services were suffering from space problems as well. The library system's crowded main reference area was contiguous to the building's major traffic path, a favorite campus walkway from the classrooms on the west and north to the Husky Union Building (HUB) on the east. This crucial library and campus information service was virtually inaccessible to individuals with disabilities. Over time, staff space had lost out to collection space. Eighty percent of the staff work stations ranged from 42 to 100 square feet, well below the state standard of 120 square feet.

All three wings of the building were unamenable to the addition of power and telecommunications to accommodate new computing and other technologies. Only one level had a network of built-in cable trays in the floors, and they were full of both used and unused cable. Any additions or changes required expensive core drilling or other structural work. Even in 1984 this obstacle was having a negative impact on services.

Boylan's report on the status of library space summarized the situation:

> The problem, simply stated, is that the libraries' facilities are generally overcrowded, over-extended, inefficient, and substandard. At recognized standards, they do not meet the requirements of the needs of a library program in a university of the quality and size of the University of Washington. . . . The continuing space problem has resulted in the libraries' current service programs operating below potential, its progress and development stultified, and its collections in jeopardy physically.

The president of the university said he found Boylan's report to be the most convincing depiction of a campus problem he had read.

Authorities Seek Site and Funding

With the university administration interested in addressing the problem, it was necessary for the library staff, campus planners, and other authorities to agree on a potential site for the new library addition. A number of possible locations on campus were examined, and Boylan led the way in preparing a selection of the most viable alternatives. Because of potential difficulties, the logical site between the HUB and the existing library—the one that was consonant with the 1915 plan—was avoided until the last possible moment. Potential problems with the site included utility structures and abandoned building foundations, a small remaining building from the Alaska–Yukon–Pacific Exposition of 1909, a dramatic loss of elevation from the front of the building to the site, and severe water drainage problems. These conditions were assumed to make construction too expensive. Another concern was that any addition large enough to solve the space problem would produce a huge library structure that, when combined with the existing 310,000 square feet, would destroy all important pedestrian pathways and, perhaps, even permanently segregate one part of the campus from the other.

Controversy regarding the site lasted for many months until the due date approached for the next biennial funding request from the university to the legislature. University government relations staff felt the time was right for proposing to the legislature a sizable allocation for the library. University administration decided to make the case immediately for a fourth wing. For lack of a more convincing idea, the new addition would be attached to the east face of the 1963 addition, ensuring expensive and problematic site preparation. Funding to renovate the first three wings would have to wait for another biennium.

As a result of a well-laid strategy on the part of the university and the excellent case for new space developed by the director of libraries, the legislature allocated $36 million that year for a new addition to the main library—at that time the largest allocation ever made for a state-funded capital project. And yet the prospects for a seamless and functional main library seemed remote. The university had chosen to acquire funding for the new construction before planning the future arrangement of the entire central library facility. To Boylan and the library staff, it seemed obvious that a structure of half a million square feet in four wings would not function well or even be very pleasing aesthetically if it were not planned from the beginning as a whole.

Bowing to the inevitable, however, Boylan set out to assist in the selection of an architect for the new wing. From that process emerged a proposal that answered many of the difficulties that university staff had pointed out concerning the HUB Yard site—and solved them brilliantly.

Architect Proposes a "Lite-Perfect" New Wing

Edward Larrabee Barnes of New York proposed an addition that included two detached segments joining at an elbow. To reduce the protrusion of the library into the HUB Yard, one segment would angle southward about 50 degrees off the main east-west axis of the library complex. Barnes took advantage of the drop in elevation from the front of the original wing to add to what he saw as a series of stepped-down peaked rooftops, hoping to suggest, both at ground level and at the skyline, something of a gabled medieval European city. In addition, Barnes's plan obscured the unpopular 1963 addition, another successful effort at achieving seamlessness.

Continuing the theme of the medieval city, Barnes proposed an arcade joining the two angled pieces of the building. With this arcade, he brought the library operation down from its height above the plaza in front of the first module to within eye-level of the campus community. He envisioned that major library services could take place in the interior spaces on either side of the arcade. Respectful of the confluence of pathways at the location of the main library, Barnes envisioned this arcade as the primary pedestrian route from the west to the east half of the campus. The only disadvantage of this decision was that it brought the number of building entrances from three to four, achieving a high degree of user convenience and acceptance that made this compromise worthwhile.

For this project Barnes moved away from his contemporary designs for corporate clients. He de-emphasized the unpopular contemporary architecture of the 1963 addition by creating an updated rendering of the Tudor Collegiate Gothic. The new addition repeats the use of the familiar brick and terra cotta in an updated fashion.

With Barnes's proposal that the new building be added to the east face of the 1963 wing, library staff imagined that the wall of the old building would in effect disappear seamlessly on every floor and that building occupants would be unaware at what point they were passing from the old building into the new. It was revealed fairly late in the design process that the seismic bracing in the 1963 wing was contained in the exterior walls. Thus, the east wall of the 1963 building could accommodate only narrow penetrations. In addition, it was discovered that the money with which to bring the old building up to date with current fire safety codes had been omitted from the budget. This required that fire doors separating the old and new buildings wherever they joined had to provide up to four hours of fire protection.

This seemed to be yet another overwhelming obstacle to a fully integrated structure. The Barnes team and Boylan developed a compromise that has proven to be successful. On each floor they incorporated at least one eight-foot penetration with four-hour fire doors, and planned the major interior pedestrian ways extending out from these openings on both the old and new sides of the wall. The remaining expanse of dividing wall on each floor was then used to house the necessary support functions—restrooms, drinking fountains, power and telecommunications closets, and photocopy centers.

Library Director and Staff Reorganize Functions

Having worked around the problem of a major dividing wall between the 1963 wing and the new addition, Boylan began to deal with the problem of arrangement of work and traffic flow among the four wings. He knew that without work on the original three wings, the logical flow of traffic and functions would be absent. Boylan used his thorough knowledge of the state budgetary process to utilize the funding to achieve his goal.

Assisted by Nancy McAdams, library architectural consultant, Boylan and library staff members proceeded to plan a reorganization of almost all functions in the main library. Their layout established logical relationships among cataloging, acquisitions, serials, reference, circulation, maps, government publications, and microforms/newspapers. Since the entire main library complex had not been planned ahead of time, any possibility of creating a gallery of library services that would extend the length of the building on the first floor could not be realized. McAdams and Boylan compensated for the inability to achieve horizontal progression of services with careful attention to the vertical placement of functions and collections. (See figures 12 through 18.)

For the new building, the Allen Library, Boylan specified that as few interior partitions as possible be included. This approach resulted in unobstructed stack floors that will be easy to reconfigure in later years if necessary, and it helped to reduce construction costs. A large subbasement space near the mechanical rooms was rough-finished for on-site storage of medium- to less-used material. It is hoped that this space will help the library staff hold the line on collection storage until technology slows the acquisition of printed material. The Allen Library provides about a dozen or more years of space at current growth rates for the libraries' collections.

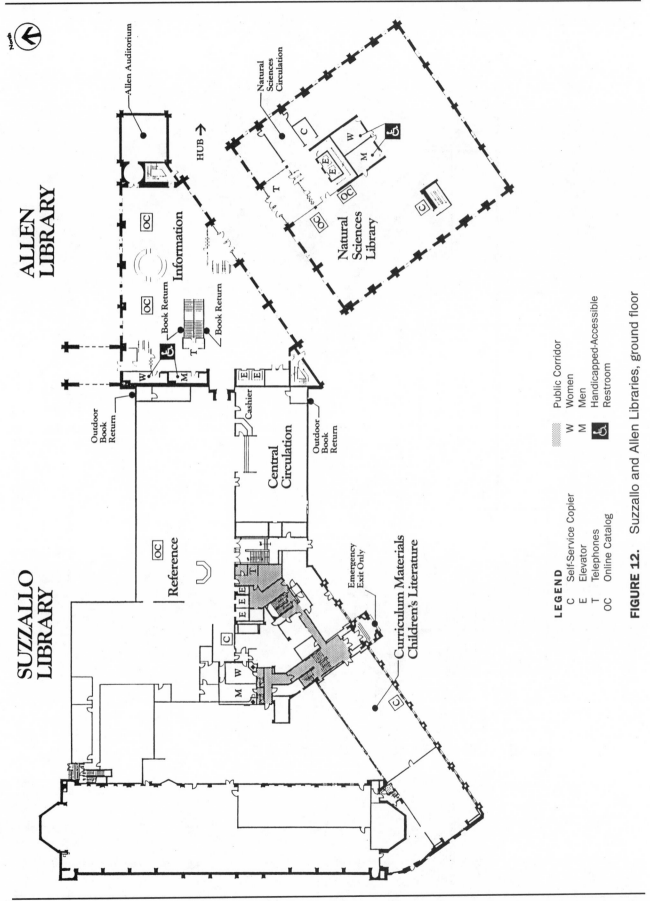

ALLEN
LIBRARY

SUZZALLO
LIBRARY

Allen Auditorium

HUB →

Information

Natural
Sciences
Circulation

Natural
Sciences
Library

Book Return

Book Return

Outdoor
Book
Return

Reference

Cashier

Central
Circulation

Outdoor
Book
Return

Emergency
Exit Only

Curriculum Materials
Children's Literature

LEGEND
C   Self-Service Copier
E   Elevator
T   Telephones
OC   Online Catalog

Public Corridor
W   Women
M   Men
Handicapped-Accessible
     Restroom

FIGURE 12.   Suzzallo and Allen Libraries, ground floor

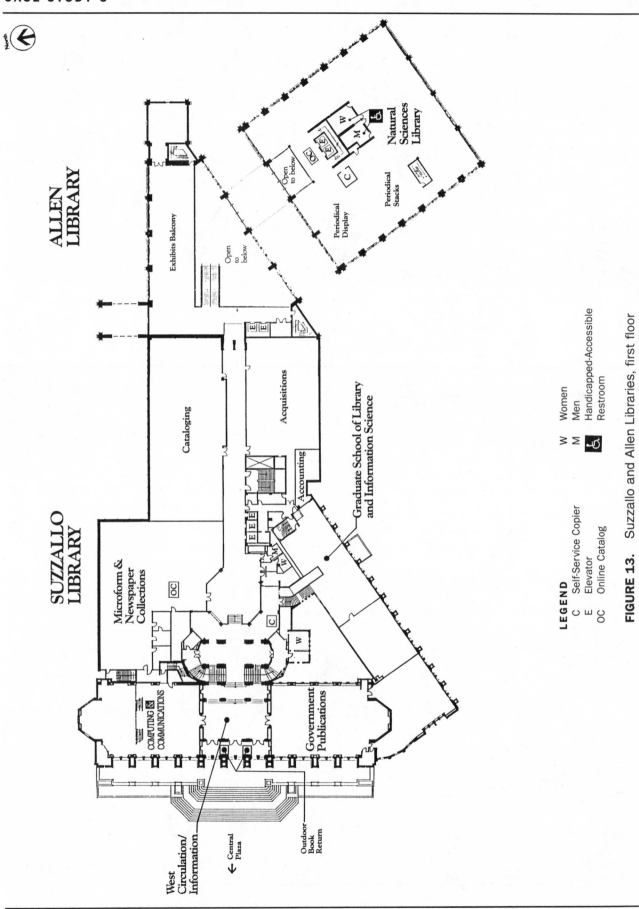

FIGURE 13. Suzzallo and Allen Libraries, first floor

LEGEND

C   Self-Service Copier
E   Elevator
OC Online Catalog

W   Women
M   Men
♿ Handicapped-Accessible
    Restroom

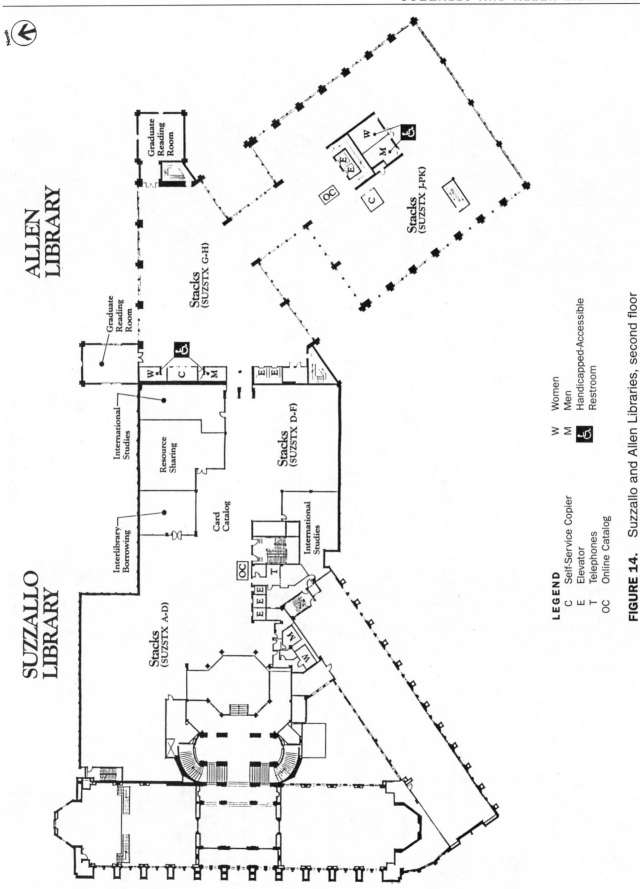

ALLEN LIBRARY

SUZZALLO LIBRARY

Graduate Reading Room

Graduate Reading Room

Stacks (SUZSTX G-H)

Stacks (SUZSTX J-PK)

Stacks (SUZSTX A-D)

Stacks (SUZSTX D-F)

International Studies

Resource Sharing

Interlibrary Borrowing

Card Catalog

International Studies

W C M

W M

E E

E E E

OC

OC

C

T

LEGEND

C Self-Service Copier
E Elevator
T Telephones
OC Online Catalog

W Women
M Men

Handicapped-Accessible Restroom

FIGURE 14. Suzzallo and Allen Libraries, second floor

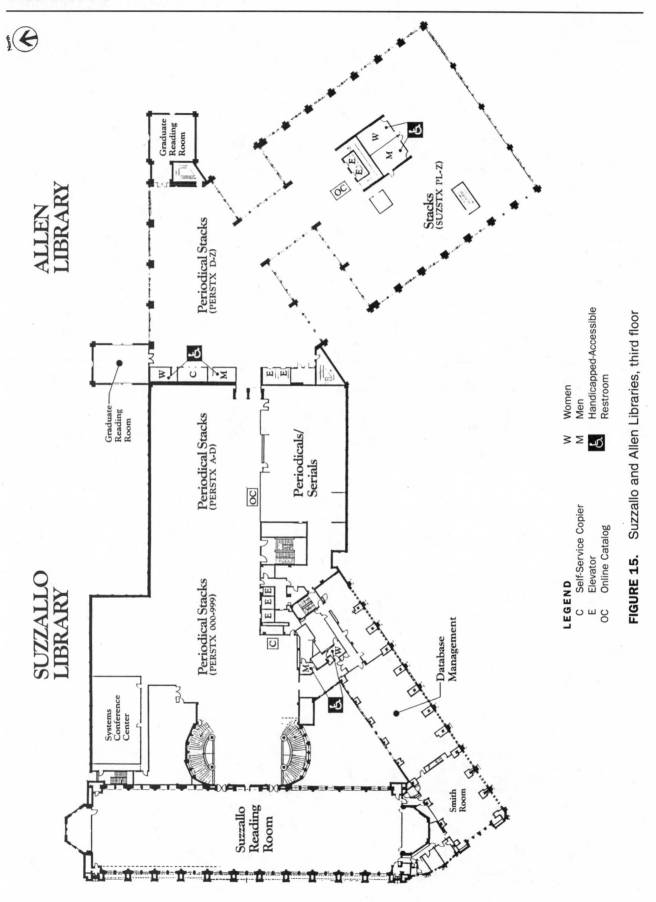

FIGURE 15. Suzzallo and Allen Libraries, third floor

LEGEND
C Self-Service Copier
E Elevator
OC Online Catalog

W Women
M Men
Handicapped-Accessible Restroom

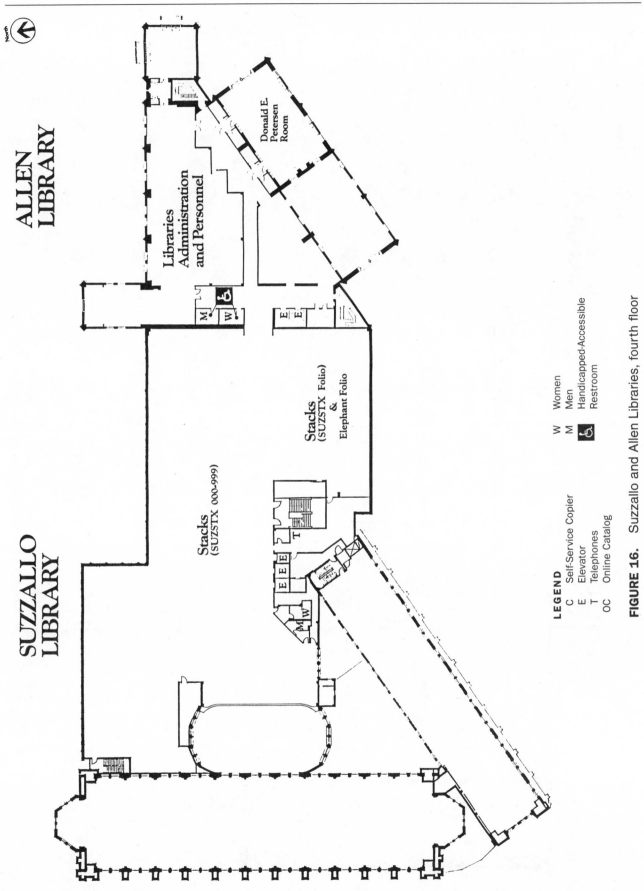

North

ALLEN LIBRARY

SUZZALLO LIBRARY

Libraries Administration and Personnel

Donald E. Petersen Room

M W

E E

Stacks (SUZSTX 000-999)

Stacks (SUZSTX Folio) & Elephant Folio

E E E

T

M W

LEGEND
C   Self-Service Copier
E   Elevator
T   Telephones
OC Online Catalog

W   Women
M   Men
♿ Handicapped-Accessible Restroom

FIGURE 16.   Suzzallo and Allen Libraries, fourth floor

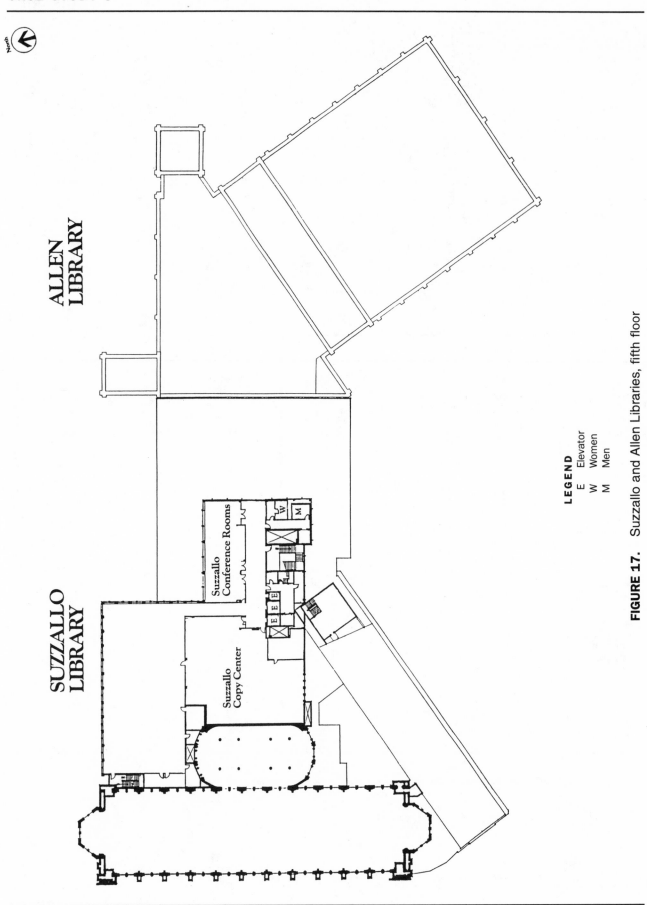

LEGEND
E Elevator
W Women
M Men

FIGURE 17. Suzzallo and Allen Libraries, fifth floor

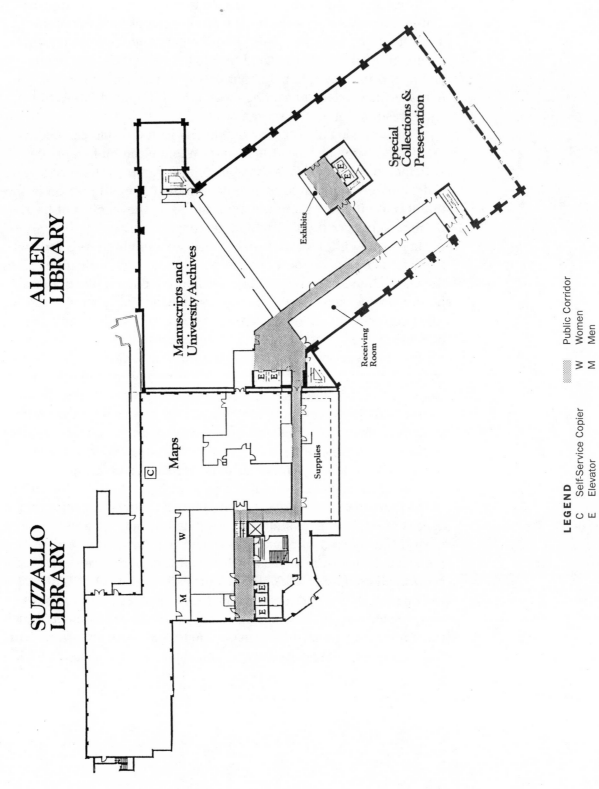

FIGURE 18. Suzzallo and Allen Libraries, basement

The Allen addition to the Suzzallo Library resulted in approximately 650 new user seats, mostly around the perimeters of the stack floors by windows. This space and arrangement, along with plenty of overhead lighting and task lights on carrels, has nearly eliminated past complaints about poorly lit user seating areas. All lights in the stacks and seating areas have ultraviolet filters to help with preservation of library materials.

This new wing also serves individuals with disabilities effectively, to a large degree because the state of Washington building codes anticipated the Americans with Disabilities Act by at least five years. Unfortunately, until large-scale renovations of the old portion of the building are funded, there will continue to be the significant barriers there to accessibility by disabled persons.

In the old building, staff spaces were reconfigured, regularizing allocations for space for work stations. Not without difficulties along the way, a building network of power and telecommunications capabilities was designed to mirror the arrangement of functions. In the Allen Library, extra-wide cable trays with four poke-throughs per bay were added in anticipation of future technology.

Positive reaction from throughout the University and the Seattle community indicates that the new structure realizes the original vision of the 1915 plan and indeed goes well beyond it. The unpopular 1963 addition is de-emphasized and now blends with the entire structure. The arcade pedestrian pathway makes an understandable transition from one portion of the campus to the other, and effectively accommodates thousands of pedestrians daily.

One of the most-important changes brought about by the siting of the fourth addition is the repositioning of the primary information access point for the main library. Walking through the arcade, members of the campus community can see the information service area immediately inside, as well as part of a current periodicals area. Eight networked computer work stations providing access to CD-ROMs, the online catalog, and locally mounted databases are also showcased inside the arcade windows. Many people have commented that the library now seems more accessible to and more integrated with the community. In short, many troublesome "seams" disappeared.

Words of Advice

Our experience in this project taught us a number of lessons that we can share.

- When the library needs space, never give up trying to demonstrate that need in order to obtain the funding for new construction or renovation no matter how discouraging the prospect of success appears. Even if it falls to a successor to actually build the new building, you will have established the necessary foundation of support for achieving the library's goal. As in our case, it can take twenty years or more. Don't be discouraged.

- Study your college or university's basic process for planning capital projects. If there is a detailed general physical development plan, learn to understand it and what the campus planners have traditionally envisioned for the library. Take into consideration such nonlibrary issues as landscaping, pedestrian and automobile traffic patterns, and the routes between receiving and service areas. Any of these, or similar issues, could become the major determiner of your building's size, shape, or location. If you understand the rationale behind campus planning decisions, you are in a better position to deal with their impact on library planning when necessary.

- Anticipate that funding can come suddenly after a long wait and that the timing will be inconvenient. As soon as you are aware that there is a space problem, initiate a detailed study. Learn the campus standards for space allocation and prepare an evaluation of the library in comparison with those standards. Keep a summary of the current numbers in your head. You will have a surprising number of opportunities to educate key members of the university community about your needs for new space.

- Learn everything you can about the existing building from roof to basement, including structural aspects, architectural style and history, and mechanical operations. This knowledge will help you interact with campus planners and architects and may help you avoid seams between the old and new space.

- If only informally, develop a master plan and a few reasonable alternatives for the existing structure and new space. If you have a vision of what the completed structure could be like, you will influence the process more effectively. On an ongoing basis, communicate this vision to library staff. An informed staff can help you educate the campus users to your needs.

- Involve as many library staff as possible and have confidence in their instincts and intuition in evaluating existing space and planning new space.

- Never stop seeking ways to economize on library space without seriously harming programs and collections. Seek new paradigms for organizing space. Include methods you have employed in your space-evaluation report. You will win regard for your efforts from the campus community, and you will strengthen your case for new space.

- Be confident in dealing with architects, engineers, contractors, and consultants. You have the experience in evaluating library needs that nonlibrary experts do not. Be willing to compromise on less-important points, especially on matters of style and design, but be true to your vision of what is best for the library.

- Finally, enjoy your project in spite of tight deadlines, late nights, bureaucratic frustrations, unfamiliar concepts, and scary decisions. Your good work will be a great gift to your institution and to the coming generations of library staff and users.

Bibliography

Boylan, Merle N. *Libraries Space Survey, 1984–2010.* Seattle, Wash.: Office of the Director, University of Washington Libraries, May 1984.

"Campus Planning During the First Century." *Washington Alumnus.* Seattle, Wash.: University of Washington Alumni Association, Winter 1963.

Jones, John Paul. *The History of the Development of the Present Campus Plan for the University of Washington.* Seattle, Wash.: University of Washington, 1940.

Menges, Gary, ed. *The Allen Library.* Seattle, Wash.: University of Washington Libraries, 1991.

Program Report. Seattle, Wash.: Ad Hoc Programming Committee for the Suzzallo Library Expansion, University of Washington Libraries, 10 June 1985.

SUMMARY

Three different libraries in three vastly different settings all faced the same problem—an increasingly pressing need for more space to house library collections, services, technology, staff, and users. However, a similar problem did not lead to similar solutions. Hope College, Western Maryland College, and the University of Washington designed plans to creatively address the issues and needs of their particular situations. And the resulting seamless addition for each library was as unique and different as each institution.

Similar themes, however, emerged in all three case studies. First was the emphasis on planning in all three cases. Library staff and architectural teams worked with dedication and determination to plan the addition thoughtfully and carefully.

Second, cooperation with campus officials echoed through all three case studies highlighting the importance of seeing the library in the larger context of the college or university and recognizing the unique role the library plays in an educational setting.

Third, no building project is without problems to be addressed, and each one of these seamless additions had their share at various stages in the process. Flexibility and creativity were evident in how the problems were addressed, whether the problem was related to site selection, elevation differences, location of public entrances, campus plans, architectural style, or impact on library services.

Finally, what is most striking in each one of these case studies is the vision that the seamless addition should, beyond all else, serve the library user better. The library staff, campus officials, and architectural teams worked to do more than add more space or build an addition for the library. Their success has defined the seamless addition.

Poster Session Abstracts

Ron G. Martin

Poster sessions on seamless library additions were presented by eight university libraries in conjunction with the 1993 American Library Association conference program sponsored by the Buildings for College and University Libraries Committee (BCUL) of the Buildings and Equipment Section (BES) of the Library Administration and Management Association (LAMA). Three of the poster sessions illustrated the three case studies presented in this publication. The abstracts presented here include a brief description of each project and a contact person.

Christopher Newport University

The Captain John Smith Library is now finishing a 20,000-square-foot addition and extensive interior renovation. The design will provide more shelving and seating space and will replace an extremely confining floor plan with a design that will allow easy reallocation of space. The architects, in consultation with library staff and an owner's committee from the university, created an open floor plan that reflected the staff's desire for flexibilty in arranging space while retaining the main entrance and lobby, which the faculty deemed important.

Contact   Wendell Barbour
Director of Library and Information Services
Christopher Newport University
Newport News, VA 23606
Phone: (804) 594-7130
Fax: (804) 594-7772
Internet: wbarbour@powhatan.cc.cnu.edu

Emory University

Emory University is planning an addition to the Woodruff Library that will function in many ways as a separate building, bridging the ravine between Woodruff (1969) and the Chandler Library (1926), the old main library on the quadrangle. The addition will be connected to Chandler both above and below grade. The facility is being designed to integrate library services with academic computing and multimedia communications services (from the campus Information Technology Division). Ground will be broken in early 1995, with an anticipated completion date of late 1996.

> *Contact*   Charles Forrest
> Director, Financial Management and Planning
> General Libraries
> Emory University
> Atlanta, GA 30322-2870
> Phone: (404) 727-0137
> Fax: (404) 727-0053
> Internet: libcgf@unix.cc.emory.edu

Hope College

In 1982 planning began at Hope College for expansion of the twenty-one-year-old library whose 245,000 volumes were housed in an area of only 37,000 square feet. The need for additional space and reorganized, easily accessible services was so extensive that a new, architecturally distinct building of 92,000 square feet was attached to the existing library. The planners, architects, and library staff worked together to create a building to provide adequate space for the growing collections, to relocate and expand services, and to establish a warm, inviting ambiance. The result—the new Van Wylen Library—has become a focal point on campus.

> *Contact*   David Jensen
> Director of Libraries
> Van Wylen Library
> Hope College
> Holland, MI 49422-9012
> Phone: (616) 394-7790
> Fax: (616) 394-7965
> Internet: jensen@hope.cit.hope.edu

Kenyon College

In March 1984 design development for an addition to the Kenyon College Library was well under way when the college president announced that the new library would be built and equipped with an Olin Foundation grant. The project was immediately faced with a new objective. It had to meet grant requirements that the new library not have a common wall with the existing library and that the new library be separately identifiable architecturally. Through careful planning and work with experienced architects, the Kenyon College Libraries now appear as two libraries from the outside while functioning as one library on the inside.

Contact   Allan W. Bosch
            Head, Humanities and Social Science Libraries
            Washington State University
            Pullman, WA 99164-5610
            Phone: (509) 335-8139
            Fax: (509) 335-6721
            Internet: bosch@wsuvm1.csc.wsu.edu

Skidmore College

Skidmore College is in the process of designing a major renovation and expansion to its existing library. Over a period of two years, the program was developed, architects were hired, and design work was begun. A key issue was identifying user needs of the existing library. A secondary issue was to reduce the two present entrances to one main library entrance. The architects and the building design committee held a series of open forums, inviting student organizations and academic departments to provide input. Skidmore's model for gathering data influenced the final design of the library renovation.

Contact   Karen A. Nuckolls
            Head, Technical Services
            Lucy Scribner Library
            Skidmore College
            Saratoga Springs, NY 12866-1632
            Phone: (518) 584-5000
            Fax: (518) 584-3023
            Internet: knuckoll@skidmore.edu

University of Oregon

The University of Oregon's Knight Library expansion and renovation project added 135,000 square feet of new space and completely renovated the existing 237,000-square-foot structure. The project's four major goals were to integrate three separate building components (1937 building plus 1950 and 1966 additions) into one functional building, to construct as much square footage as possible for readers and storage, to develop a flexible design to allow response to change and service capacity into the twenty-first century, and to recognize the building's historic and symbolic role on the campus.

Contact   Andrew Bonamici
Assistant University Librarian for Administrative
    Services
University of Oregon Library
Eugene, OR 97403-1299
Phone: (503) 346-2682
Fax: (503) 346-3094
Internet: bonamici@oregon.uoregon.edu

University of Washington

Severe space shortages in the University of Washington's Suzzallo Library created a need for more space in the main library to house the growing humanities and social science collections as well as to provide adequate space for staff and readers. As a result of a favorable legislative climate and excellent planning on the part of the university and library administrations, a $36 million allocation was approved by the state legislature and the Kenneth S. Allen Library addition at the University of Washington was constructed. The Allen addition increased the square footage of the existing Suzzallo Library to 510,000 square feet, spread over four wings. Despite a series of site and building design problems, library staff worked with architects and planners to create a seamless addition and reorganized nearly all the functions of the main library to establish a more-logical arrangement.

Contact   Sarah C. Michalak
Assistant Director of Libraries, Library Development
    and Planning
University of Washington Libraries

Libraries Administration
Allen Library, Room 482, FM-25
Seattle, WA 98195
Phone: (206) 685-1973 or 543-1760
Fax: (206) 685-8727
Internet: michalak@u.washington.edu

Western Maryland College

The design goal for the Hoover Library was to provide a seamless
union of new and old construction with a floor plan that would function as a whole. The seamless addition doubled the size of the
library, established a study environment of recognized excellence,
and accommodated emerging information technologies. The addition was completed in 1991, and renovation of the original building
was completed at the end of the year.

Contact   Dave Neikirk
Library Director
Hoover Library
Western Maryland College
2 College Hill
Westminster, MD 21157-4390
Phone: (410) 857-2281
Fax: (410) 857-2748
Internet: hneikirk@cap.gwu.edu

APPENDIX B

Checklist of Additions
to Academic Library Buildings

Nancy McAdams

In conjunction with the conference program entitled "Planning Academic Library Building Additions: A Seamless Approach," information on recently completed or in-progress additions to academic library buildings was compiled in a checklist format by Nancy McAdams of McAdams Planning Consultants, Inc., of Austin, Texas. The checklist was updated for this book and is provided here as an additional source of information and contacts for librarians planning a library building program or addition. Address lists of library contacts and architectural firms associated with the additions appear following the checklist. Where more than one architectural firm is associated with a project, each is listed individually in alphabetical order.

Addition and Renovation Completed

Institution and Library	Location	Date Completed	Project Size (in thousands) Addition	Project Size (in thousands) Total Bldg.	Approximate Cost (in millions)	Library Contact*	Architects*
Berea College Hutchins Library	Berea, Ky.	1991	30 gsf	98 gsf	$ 5	Kirk	Johnson/Romanowitz
Hope College Van Wylen Library	Holland, Mich.	1988	80 gsf	92 gsf	$ 8.5	Jensen	Shepley
Mount Holyoke College College Library	South Hadley, Mass.	1990 1992	58 gsf	116 gsf	$13.8	Edmonds	Gund
North Carolina State U. D. H. Hill Library	Raleigh, N.C.	1990	107 gsf	344 gsf	$ 9.3	Keener	ENG/SIX
Northern Arizona U. Cline Library	Flagstaff, Ariz.	1992	120 gsf	210 gsf	$16.6	Collins	Roberts/ Dinsmore and Sasaki (Watertown)
Oakland U. Kresge Library	Rochester, Mich.	1989	88 gsf	165 gsf	$ 9	Frankie	Rossetti
Princeton U. Firestone Library	Princeton, N.J.	1988	50 gsf	415 gsf	$13.8	Pearson	Koetter
Stephen F. Austin U. Ralph W. Steen Library	Nacogdoches, Tex.	1992	105 gsf	245 gsf	$10.5	Cage	Marsellos
U. of California, San Diego Central Library	La Jolla, Calif.	1993	137 asf	260 asf	$36.5	Mirsky	Birkerts and BSHA
Western Maryland College Hoover Library	Westminster, Md.	1991	57 gsf	74 gsf	$ 8	Neikirk	Hillier

Notes: * See following alphabetical listings with addresses
asf = assignable square feet
gsf = gross square feet
na = not available

Addition Completed, Renovation in Progress

Institution and Library	Location	Date Completed	Project Size (in thousands)		Approximate Cost (in millions)	Library Contact*	Architects*
			Addition	Total Bldg.			
Cornell U. Carl A. Kroch Library (Olin Library)	Ithaca, N.Y.	1992 addn.	97 gsf	340 gsf	$25	Hoffman	Shepley
Rutgers U. Alexander Library	New Brunswick, N.J.	1993 addn.	48 asf	188 asf	$16.5	Gaunt	Hillier
U. of California, Davis Peter J. Shields Library	Davis, Calif.	1990 addn.	184 gsf	386 gsf	$36.5	Bynon	Simon
U. of Washington Kenneth S. Allen Library	Seattle, Wash.	1990	220 gsf	530 gsf	$23	Michalak	Barnes

Addition under Construction

Institution and Library	Location	Project Size (in thousands)		Approximate Cost (in millions)	Library Contact*	Architects*
		Addition	Total Bldg.			
Eastern Kentucky U. John Grant Crabbe Library	Richmond, Ky.	81 gsf	na	$11.7	Myers	Sherman
Northern Kentucky U. W. Frank Steely Library	Highland Hgts., Ky.	53 gsf	120 gsf	$ 9.1	Winner	Godsey
U. of California, Berkeley Doe and Moffitt Libraries	Berkeley, Calif.	183 gsf	405 gsf	$36	Yasaki	Esherick
U. of Maryland, Baltimore County Albin O. Kuhn Library	Baltimore, Md.	132 gsf	278 gsf	$19	LeBreton	Shepley and Cho

Notes: * See following alphabetical listings with addresses
asf = assignable square feet
gsf = gross square feet
na = not available

Addition Being Designed or Construction Documents Being Prepared

Institution and Library	Location	Project Size (in thousands)		Approximate Cost (in millions)	Library Contact*	Architects*
		Addition	Total Bldg.			
Cornell U. Catherwood Library	Ithaca, N.Y.	28 asf	58 asf	Part of larger project	Hoffmann	Beckhard
Cornell U. Mann Library	Ithaca, N.Y.	75 asf	176 asf	$34	Schrempf	Barnes
Emory U. Woodruff/Chandler Library	Atlanta, Ga.	80 gsf	375 gsf	$24	Forrest	Shepley
Kansas State U. Farrell Library	Manhattan, Kans.	153 gsf	350 gsf	$28	Hobrock	BBA and Hammond
Oregon State U. Central Library	Corvallis, Ore.	123 gsf	188 gsf	$30	George	SRG and Sasaki (SF)
Texas A and M U. Library, Computing, Study Complex	College Station, Tex.	63 asf	415 asf	na	Thornton	Graeber
U. of California, Los Angeles Southern Regional Library Facility	Los Angeles, Calif.	88 asf	191 asf	$14.8	Bellanti	Leidenfrost and Israel
U. of Hawaii Hamilton Library	Honolulu, Hawaii	166 gsf	446 gsf	$74	Watson	Matsushita
U. of Utah Marriott Library	Salt Lake City, Utah	209 gsf	495 gsf	$34	Hanson	Birkerts and BSHA

Notes: * See following alphabetical listings with addresses
asf = assignable square feet
gsf = gross square feet
na = not available

Programming Completed

Institution and Library	Location	Project Size (in thousands) Addition	Total Bldg.	Approximate Cost (in millions)	Library Contact*	Architects*
Pennyslvania State U. Pattee Library	University Park, Pa.	132 gsf	366 gsf	$25	Dow	Celli-Flynn

Preliminary Planning Begun

Institution and Library	Location	Project Size (in thousands) Addition	Total Bldg.	Approximate Cost (in millions)	Library Contact*	Architects*
Rice U. Fondren Library	Houston, Tex.	36 asf	201 asf	na	Shapiro	Not yet selected
San Francisco State U. J. Paul Leonard Library	San Francisco, Calif.	100 gsf	287 gsf	na	Dobb	TAC Preliminary study
U. of California, Santa Cruz McHenry Library	Santa Cruz, Calif.	85 asf	200 asf	$30	White	Not yet selected

Notes: * See following alphabetical listings with addresses
asf = assignable square feet
gsf = gross square feet
na = not available

Library Contacts

Bellanti
Claire Bellanti, Director
UC Southern Regional Library Facility
405 Hilgard Avenue
Los Angeles, CA 90024-1388
Phone: (310) 206-2010
Fax: (310) 206-5074
Internet: ecz5cqb@mvs.oac.ucla.edu

Bynon
George E. Bynon, Assistant University
   Librarian
Shields Library
University of California, Davis
Davis, CA 95616
Phone: (916) 752-2259
Fax: (916) 752-6899
Internet: gebynon@ucdavis.edu

Cage
Al Cage, Director
Steen Library, Stephen F. Austin State
   University
Box 13055, SFA Station
Nacogdoches, TX 75962-3055
Phone: (409) 568-1414
Fax: (409) 568-4117

Collins
Jean D. Collins, Dean and University
   Librarian
Cline Library
Northern Arizona University
Flagstaff, AZ 86011-6022
Phone: (602) 523-6801
Fax: (602) 523-3770

Dobb
Linda S. Dobb, Associate University Librarian
San Francisco State University
1630 Holloway Avenue
San Francisco, CA 94127
Phone: (415) 338-2011
Fax: (415) 338-6199

Dow
Ronald F. Dow, Associate Dean
Pattee Library
Pennsylvania State University
University Park, PA 16802
Phone: (814) 865-0401
Fax: (814) 865-3665
Internet: rfd@psulias.psu.bitnet

Edmonds
Anne C. Edmonds, College Librarian
Williston Memorial Library
Mount Holyoke College
South Hadley, MA 01075
Phone: (413) 538-2225
Internet: ace@mhc.mtholyoke.edu

Forrest
Charles Forrest, Director, Financial
   Management and Planning
Woodruff Library
Emory University
Atlanta, GA 30322-2870
Phone: (404) 727-0137
Fax: (404) 727-0805
Internet: libcgf@unix.cc.emory.edu

Note: Addresses provided by respondents..

Frankie
Suzanne O. Frankie, Dean of Libraries
Oakland University
Rochester, MI 48309-4401
Phone: (313) 370-2486
Fax: (313) 370-2458

Gaunt
Marianne I. Gaunt, Associate Librarian
Alexander Library, Rutgers University
169 College Avenue
New Brunswick, NJ 08903
Phone: (908) 932-7505
Fax: (908) 932-7637
Internet: gaunt@zodiac.rutgers.edu

George
Melvin R. George, University Librarian
Oregon State University
Corvallis, OR 97331
Phone: (508) 737-1308
Fax: (508) 737-3453
Internet: georgem@ccmail.orst.edu

Hanson
Roger K. Hanson, Director of Libraries
Marriott Library
University of Utah
Salt Lake City, UT 84112
Phone: (801) 581-8558
Fax: (801) 585-3464

Hobrock
Brice Hobrock, Dean of Libraries
Farrell Library
Kansas State University
Manhattan, KS 66506
Phone: (913) 532-7404
Fax: (913) 532-6144
Internet: hobrock@ksuvm.ksu.edu

Hoffmann
John Hoffmann, Director of Facilities Planning
213 Olin Library
Cornell University
Ithaca, NY 14853
Phone: (607) 255-5068
Fax: (607) 255-9346
Internet: jah9@cornell.edu

Jensen
David Jensen, Director
Van Wylen Library
Hope College
Holland, MI 49422-9012
Phone: (616) 395-7790
Fax: (616) 394-7965
Internet: jensend@hope.cit.hope.edu

Keener
D. S. Keener, Associate Director for
    Administration
North Carolina State University Libraries
Box 7111
Raleigh, NC 27695-7111
Phone: (919) 515-2843
Fax: (919) 515-3628

Kirk
Thomas G. Kirk, College Librarian
Hutchins Library
Berea College
Berea, KY 40404
Phone: (606) 986-9341
Fax: (606) 986-9494
Internet: bertgk@ukpr.uky.edu

LeBreton
Jonathan LeBreton, Assistant Director
Albin O. Kuhn Library 106B
University of Maryland Baltimore County
Baltimore, MD 21228
Phone: (410) 455-2356
Fax: (410) 455-1078

Michalak
Sarah C. Michalak, Assistant Director
  of Libraries
Allen Library FM-25
University of Washington
Seattle, WA 98195
Phone: (206) 685-1973
Fax: (206) 685-8727
Internet: michalak@u.washington.edu

Mirsky
Phyllis S. Mirsky
Central Library 0175G
University of California, San Diego
La Jolla, CA 92093-0175
Phone: (619) 534-1235
Internet: psmirsky@ucsd.edu

Myers
Marcia Myers, Director of Libraries
John Grant Crabbe Library
Eastern Kentucky University
Richmond, KY 40475-3121
Phone: (606) 622-1778
Fax: (606) 622-1174

Neikirk
Dave Neikirk, Director
Hoover Library
Western Maryland College
Westminster, MD 21157
Phone: (410) 857-2281
Fax: (410) 857-2748
Internet: hneikirk@cap.gwu.edu

Pearson
Dorothy Pearson, Associate University
  Librarian
Firestone Library
One Washington Road
Princeton, NJ 08544
Phone: (609) 258-3215
Fax: (609) 258-4105

Schrempf
Peter Schrempf, Administrative Manager
Mann Library
Cornell University
Ithaca, NY 14853
Phone: (607) 255-2285
Fax: (607) 255-0850
Internet: pfsi@cornell.edu

Shapiro
Beth J. Shapiro, University Librarian
Fondren Library
Rice University
P.O. Box 1892
Houston, TX 77251-1892
Phone: (713) 527-4022
Fax: (713) 285-5258

Thornton
Joyce K. Thornton, Executive Assistant
Sterling C. Evans Library
Texas A and M University
College Station, TX 77843-5000
Phone: (409) 862-4232
Fax: (409) 845-6238
Internet: jkthorn@tamu.edu

Watson
Joyce Watson, Building Planning Coordinator
Hamilton Library, University of Hawaii
2550 The Mall
Honolulu, HI 96822
Phone: (808) 956-2771
Fax: (808) 956-5968
Internet: joycew@uhunix.bitnet

White
Robert L. White, Assistant University Librarian
McHenry Library
University of California, Santa Cruz
Santa Cruz, CA 95064
Phone: (408) 459-2076
Fax: (408) 459-8206
Internet: rlwhite@scilibx.ucsc.edu

Winner
Marian C. Winner, Director
W. Frank Steely Library
Northern Kentucky University
Nunn Drive
Highland Heights, KY 41099
Phone: (606) 572-5483
Fax: (606) 572-5390

Yasaki
Fred Yasaki, Library Architect
Doe Library, Room 188
University of California, Berkeley
Berkeley, CA 94720
Phone: (510) 642-5154
Fax: (510) 643-7891

Architects

Barnes
Edward Larrabee Barnes/John M. Y. Lee
    and Partners
320 W. Thirteenth Street
New York, NY 10014

BBA
Brent Bowman and Associates
    Architects
228 Poyntz Avenue
Manhattan, KS 66502-0023

Beckhard
Herbert Beckhard, Frank Richlan and
    Associates
333 Seventh Avenue
New York, NY 10001

Birkerts
Gunnar Birkerts and Associates, Inc.
292 Harmon Street
Birmingham, MI 48009-3800

BSHA
BSHA Inc.
329 Fourth Avenue, #200
San Diego, CA 92101-6123

Celli-Flynn
Celli-Flynn and Associates
606 Liberty Avenue
Pittsburgh, PA 15222

Cho
Cho, Wilks and Benn Inc.
218 W. Saratoga Street
Baltimore, MD 21234

ENG/SIX
ENG/SIX Associates
1095 Hendersonville Road
Asheville, NC 28803

Homsey
Esherick Homsey Dodge and Davis
2789 Twenty-fifth Street, 3rd floor
San Francisco, CA 94110-3597

Godsey
Godsey Associates Architects
629 Fourth Avenue, Suite 400
Louisville, KY 40202-2461

Graeber
Graeber, Simmons and Cowan AIA
    Architects, Inc.
211 E. Seventh Street, Suite 300
Austin, TX 78701

Gund
Graham Gund Architects Inc.
47 Thorndike Street
Cambridge, MA 02141

Hammond
Hammond Beeby and Babka, Inc.
440 N. Wells, Suite 630
Chicago, IL 60610

Hillier
The Hillier Group
500 Alexander Park, CN-23
Princeton, NJ 08543-0023

Israel
Franklin D. Israel Design Associates
254 S. Robertson Boulevard
Beverly Hills, CA 90211

Johnson/Romanowitz
Johnson/Romanowitz Architects, Inc.
222 E. Vine Street
Lexington, KY 40507

Koetter
Koetter Kim and Associates
344 Boylston Street
Boston, MA 02116

Leidenfrost
Leidenfrost, Horowitz and Associates
1833 Victory Boulevard
Glendale, CA 91201-2557

Marsellos
Marsellos and Scott, Architects
   and Engineers
404 Perry Building
Lufkin, TX 75901

Matsushita
Matsushita, Saito and Associates
1580 Makaloa Street
Honolulu, HI 96814-3237

Roberts/Dinsmore
Roberts/Dinsmore Associates
426 N. Forty-fourth Street, Suite 100
Phoenix, AZ 85008-6595

Rossetti
Rossetti Associates/ Architects Planners
601 Washington Boulevard
Detroit, MI 48226

Sasaki (SF)
Sasaki Associates, Inc.
444 DeHaro Street, #202
San Francisco, CA 94107

Sasaki (Watertown)
Sasaki Associates, Inc.
64 Pleasant Street
Watertown, MA 02172

Shepley
Shepley Bulfinch Richardson and Abbott Inc.
40 Broad Street
Boston, MA 02109

Sherman
Sherman Carter Barnhart Architects
1900 Lexington Financial Center
Lexington, KY 40507-1326

Simon
Simon Martin-Vegue Winkelstein Moris
501 Second Street, Suite 701
San Francisco, CA 94107-1431

SRG
SRG Partnership P.C. Architects & Planners
621 S.W. Morrison, Suite 200
Portland, OR 97205

TAC
The Architects Collaborative
649 Front Street
San Francisco, CA 94111

Note: Addresses compiled from *ProFile: The Official Directory of the American Institute of Architects, 1991–92,* 7th ed. (Topeka, Kans.: Archimedia, 1991).

APPENDIX C

Bibliography of Related ALA/LAMA Publications

Librarians planning a library building project may be interested in a number of related publications of the Library Administration and Management Association of the American Library Association.

Dahlgren, Anders, and Erla Beck, eds. *Planning Library Buildings: A Select Bibliography.* Chicago: American Library Association, 1990.

Dailey, Kazuko, ed. *Library Buildings Consultants List.* Chicago: American Library Association, 1993.

Martin, Ron G., ed. *Libraries for the Future: Planning Buildings That Work.* Proceedings of the Library Buildings Preconference, June 27–28, 1991, in Atlanta, Georgia. Chicago: American Library Association, 1992.

Sannwald, William W., ed. *Checklist of Library Building Design Considerations.* Chicago: American Library Association, 1991.

Smith, Lester K., ed. *Planning Library Buildings: From Decision to Design.* Chicago: American Library Association, 1986.